A BIBLIOGRAPHY OF FIGURE SKATING

THE INTERNATIONAL GUIDE TO READING ABOUT THE WORLD'S MOST EXCITING SPORT

Ryan Stevens

Canadian Cataloguing in Publication Data

Title: A Bibliography of Figure Skating: The International Guide To Reading About The World's Most Exciting Sport
Author: Stevens, Ryan, 1982-
Independently published
ISBN: 978-1-7381982-1-4

Copyright © 2023
by Ryan Stevens

Independently published
All rights reserved

Every reasonable effort has been made to cite and/or credit all source material included in this book.

If errors or omissions have occurred, they will be corrected in future editions provided written notification and supporting documentation has been received by the author.

TABLE OF CONTENTS

Introduction	1
The Treasure Hunt	3
The First Bibliography of Skating	8
Books	12
Newspapers	253
Periodicals	256
Acknowledgments	280
Author's Note	281
Other Books	282

INTRODUCTION

Many of us walk around with smartphones in our pockets, harbouring the assumption that every fact we need to know about figure skating is only a click away. It couldn't be further from the truth. The fact is, there is always more to know about the world's most exciting sport and much of that knowledge simply can't be found online.

There are a laundry list of reasons why Google isn't always going to provide you with all of the information about figure skating you might be looking for.

Wikipedia may seem like a good starting point but, owing to its very design, it is highly unreliable. Absolutely anyone can edit it and put whatever they want.. The volunteers overseeing edits generally have do not have the skating background to know the difference between fact and fiction.

There are some great, well-researched skating blogs and podcasts out there. There are also others which rely more on rumour mills than primary sources. YouTube plays host to thousands of videos of figure skating performances, but some videos come down almost as quickly as they go up due to copyright issues.

If there's one thing I have learned from researching figure skating history over the last decade, it is that your understanding of the sport will always be richer if you open your eyes to the wonderful world of skating books, magazines, newspapers and journals around you and don't rely solely on online sources.

There are so many treasures hiding in plain sight and the goal of this bibliography of skating is to lead you straight to them.

3

THE TREASURE HUNT

Before we explore the wonderful world of figure skating in print, I want to talk about the obvious problem when it comes to tracking down books and periodicals - many of which are long out of print... how to find them!

Libraries and Archives

Libraries and archives should always be the first place you look for a book. Not only are you doing Marie Kondo proud by saving a little space on your bookshelves, but you are tapping into resources that are much more extensive than you might realize.

Start by doing a general search on figure skating at your local library and seeing what may come up. If your library also plays host to a Local History Room, I would also do a search there, as you well find books or periodicals relating to skating clubs or athletes in your own area.

Whatever you can't find, your librarian may well be able to track down for you. I can't tell you how many rare, hard-to-find skating books I've got my hands on through inter-library loans. These loans are often free or quite inexpensive.

You also visit local archives or do a search online to see if other archives in your country may have a book or magazine in their holdings. The Digital Public Library of

America, Library and Archives Canada, National Library of Australia, Bildarchiv (Austria), National Archives (UK) are all great starting points in this regard. If you are in Canada, there are several major collections in libraries and archives that may be of great interest:

Frances Dafoe fonds - York University Libraries
Skating Collection at McMaster University
Skating Collections at The ArQuives – Canada's LGBTQ2+ Archives
1996 World Figure Skating Championships fonds - City of Edmonton Archives

Private Collections

There are a surprising number of people with extensive collections of skating books, magazines and ephemera throughout the world. Roy Blakey's Ice Stage Archive, based down in the States, is perhaps the most impressive.

Ask around and see if anyone in your sphere may know a skating collector. Your skating club may even have a stash of old skating books and magazines collecting dust in a box in someone's basement and not realize it.

The vast majority of people who collect skating memorabilia are absolutely delightful and would be more than happy to share information with you if they have access to it. You never know until you ask!

EBay

Hit and miss is the best phrase to use when describing the experience of shopping for skating books and magazines on EBay. Many people, either out of sentimentality or greed, tend to overvalue the skating memorabilia they sell on there. For the love of Michelle Kwan, do not spend $30.00 plus shipping on one skating magazine. Try searching for 'lots' or 'bundles', where someone is selling various skating books or ephemera in one go. It's better value for money. Most people going this route just want to see what they have go to a good home for a fair price. If you are buying anything from out of country on EBay through the Global Shipping Program, factor in the possibility of additional customs fees when you decide whether or not to make your purchase.

Online Retailers

Never count out online retailers when it comes to finding skating books. They are a great way of finding not only new releases, but many books from other countries that are harder to find in North America. If you have a particular book in mind, take a look and see if it is listed on your favourite book retailer's site. Snag a copy of "The Almanac of Canadian Figure Skating" or "Technical Merit: A History of Figure Skating Jumps" while you are at it... you won't be disappointed!

Used Bookstores

Used bookstores can be an absolute gold mine when it

comes to tracking down skating books and magazines. Start by shopping local. Pop in to your friendly neighbourhood bookseller and see if they've got any skating books collecting dust.

If you want to go the online route, Thriftbooks, AbeBooks and Biblio are all excellent sites. The latter often runs sales for 10-15% off if you buy multiple books at the same time. Many small used bookstores around the world are affiliated with Biblio in some way, shape or form, so by shopping there, you are still supporting small, local businesses.

Yard Sales and Estate Auctions

If you find yourself at a yard sale or estate auction, there's always a small chance you might find an old skating book or show program among the items being sold. You never know what treasures may have been hiding in someone's attic or basement just waiting to be discovered by you. Skating figurines, sheet music, trade cards, pins and badges are all very collectible.

Free Online Libraries

The fact that many old skating publications may be found on Google Books may not be a surprise to anyone, but did you know that there are several other places online where you can read dozens upon dozens of great skating books for free?

Start with The Internet Archive, a non-profit online

library, where you can borrow millions of free books. Then check out the University of Connecticut's Digital Collections. Their Skating Collection consists of over three hundred digitized skating books, donated by the late Richard Stephenson of Storrs, Connecticut. Europeana and Gallica also boast impressive collections. Broaden your search results by searching not only for skating books, but for books labelled "winter sports".

The World Figure Skating Museum

Richard Stephenson also donated many items from his massive personal collection to the World Figure Skating Museum in Colorado Springs.

The Museum's Archives consist of over three thousand items, including numerous skating books and complete sets of skating magazines from both North America and Europe. Anyone is welcome to make an appointment to study anything in the Collection by reaching out to the Museum's Archivist.

Now that you have some ideas about how you can track down the books and magazines highlighted in this book, I want to talk a little bit about the first Bibliography of Skating and the Victorian man who created it. You might call it this book's prequel!

FREDERICK FOSTER AND THE FIRST BIBLIOGRAPHY OF SKATING

Frederick William Foster was born on September 26, 1849 in Camberwell, Surrey, England. His father Erasmus Robert Foster was the Resident Director of the Britannia Mutual Life Association. His mother Eliza Bevington was the daughter of the owner of the famous leather manufacturing firm of Bevington and Sons, operated out of Neckinger Mills in Bermondsey.

When Frederick came of age, he joined the family leather business, working his way up from being a tanner's assistant to taking on a managerial position. In 1899, he married Alice Neill, whose family came from the Cape Colony, in what is now South Africa. Soon after, Frederick and his wife were blessed with a son and daughter.

Sadly, Frederick fell on hard times during the early Edwardian era and was forced to let his three servants go and give up his home. He passed away at the age of fifty-seven in Hackney, Middlesex in 1905. His wife moved to North Croydon to raise their children under the roof of her brother and sister-in-law. Frederick's son William Neill 'Bonzo' Foster was inducted as a

Commander of the Order of the British Empire (CBE) for his work in the petroleum industry in Trinidad in 1958.

Very much a Renaissance man in his lifetime, Frederick was an admirer of English Romantic poet Percy Bysshe Shelley and member of The Shelley Society. He served as the London agent for Harold Fielding-Hall, a high-ranking colonial official stationed in Upper Burma who wrote several books on Buddhism. He was also a voracious reader, talented writer and keen skating enthusiast.

Frederick started compiling a bibliography of books and articles about skating in the early 1870's, first publishing them as a tiny column in Oxford University's journal "Notes and Queries" in March of 1874. By 1881, he had amassed a list of one hundred and twenty-six books relating to ice skating, and many more on early bone and snow skates. Expanded versions of his bibliography were published in subsequent issues of "Notes and Queries", with more extensive versions printed in "The Bibliographer" in 1883 and 1884. Around the same time, he was also writing articles on skating himself for "Bell's Life in London and Sporting Chronicle".

Frederick did not have the luxury of utilizing the internet when he compiled his bibliography of skating. His list grew by appealing to readers of "Notes and Queries", corresponding by letter with Eugene Beauharnais Cook, a talented skater and chess enthusiast, and consulting with speed skating and bandy authority Charles Goodman Tebbutt. A trip to the Paris library which is now the Bibliothèque nationale de France greatly enriched his research.

In March of 1898, Frederick's "A Bibliography of Skating" was privately printed by Lord Charles Beresford's Private Secretary Benjamin Webber Warhurst, Esq. in St. Paulton's Square, Chelsea, London.

The volume never would have made it to print without the support and co-operation of England's National Skating Association and the IEV (ISU). Dr. George Herbert Fowler, the NSA's ISU Delegate, suggested they invite the other IEV member federations to officially subscribe for copies of the book at five shillings a pop. Over a century before Kickstarter was conceived, crowdfunding was very much alive and well in the skating world.

When the book came out, it was reviewed in the "Field: The Country Gentleman's Newspaper", a widely circulated and highly-regarded hobby magazine. The reviewer wrote, "To anyone interested in the subject, the compilation really possesses much interest, and it is far from being such a dry-as-dust affair as might pardonably be supposed. All the byeways of literature, however unpromising they may appear to have been, have been traversed for material, and the compiler has known how to extract the kernel of references to skating and allied matters, and it is these extracts which make the book interesting as well as useful."

It is my sincere hope that this niche book, picking up in 1898 where the late Frederick William Foster's ended off, proves to be interesting and useful in its own right.

BOOKS

This bibliography of skating is not meant to be exhaustive – but it is as thorough as a good technical specialist making an edge call. If I failed to include a book, that doesn't necessarily mean it's not a great one.

GENERAL

This listing of general books about figure skating includes instructional and educational books and books that combine a mix of history, educational and instructional material with photos, interviews, etc.

Most rulebooks and other educational materials presented by the ISU and various national skating associations are not included, though they are a valuable source of information.

Combined Figure Skating
George Wood
1899, English Style focus

A Lesson in Skating
George A. Meagher
1900

Principle of Skating Turns
Henry C. Lowther
1900, English Style focus

A Handbook of Figure Skating for Use on the Ice

George Henry Browne
1900, further editions released 1904, 1907, 1913

Фигурное катание на коньках
L.A. Walter
1900, Russian language book

Klizanje
Franjo Bučar
1901, Croatian language book

W. Swatek's Schlittschuhlauf Figuren
Robert Holletschek, W. Swatek
1901, German language book

Skating, Figure-Skating
John Moyer Heathcote, C..G. Tebbutt, T. Maxwell Witham
1901, previous editions published in 1892 and third edition released in 1902, English Style focus

Edges and Striking
Henry C. Lowther
1902, English Style focus

English Skating In Three Parts
Henry C. Lowther
1902, English Style focus

Combined Figure-Skating
Henry C. Lowther
1902, English Style focus

English Sport
Alfred E.T. Watson
1903, chapter on skating by the Countess of Minto

Combined Hand-In-Hand Figure-Skating
N.G. Thompson, Fanny Laura Cannan, Viscount Doneraile
1904, English Style focus

Figure Skating
Herbert Ramon Yglesias
1905, further editions published in 1914, 1930, 1933, 1940

Der Wintersport
J., W. and Fr. Scheibert
1905, German language book

Die Kunst des Schlittschuhlaufens
Franz Calistus
1905, German language book (original version published in 1890)

Handbok i konståkning på skridskor
Ulrich Salchow
1906

Leiddraad bij de beoefening ven de beginselen van het schoon- en kunstrijden
Dr. J.A. Schutter
1907, Dutch language book

Luistelu: neuvoja luistelutaidon alkeissa
Yrjö Weilin
1907, Finnish language book

Figure Skating
Edgar Syers
1908

English Figure Skating: A Guide to the Theory and Practice of Skating in the English Style
E.F. Benson
1908, English Style focus

Auf dem Eise: Leichtverständliche Anleitung für Herren, Damen und Kinder, es im Schlittschuhlaufen sehr bald zur höchsten Vollendung zu bringen
Alfred R. Seifert
1908, German language book

Paarlaufen und Gruppenlaufen auf dem Eise
George Helfrich
1908, German language book with a focus on pairs skating

Valsing on Ice Described & Analysed with Hints for Attaining Proficiency in the Art Together with the Rules & Regulations For Competition Adopted by Prince's Skating Club
Ernest Law
1908, later released in 1910

氷滑術初歩
Kiichi Yamamoto
1909, Japanese language book

Figures of the Second Class Test
Arthur Hadley
1910

Winter in der Schweiz: Wintersport und Winterkuren
Jakob Christoph Heer, Edwin Furrer
1910, focus on winter sports resorts in Switzerland with mention of skating events held at each

Le Patinage à glace et à roulettes
Paul Bonhomme
1910, French language book

The "New" Skating: International Style of Ancient Greek Form, of Early American Invention, of Late European Development: The International System Newly Expounded and Adapted to American Conditions (later released as "A Skating Primer")
George Henry Browne
1910, second edition in 1912

Les Sports d'hiver
Louis Magnus, Renaud de La Fregeolière
1911, French language book

Eissport und Eisspiele
Walter Hammer
1911, German language book

Haandbok i Kunstløp paa skøiter: enkeltløp og parløp
Yngvar Bryn
1911, Norwegian language book

A Book of Winter Sports: An Attempt to Catch the Spirit of the Keen Joys of the Winter Season
J.C. Dier
1912

氷滑
Shirō Kawakubo
1912, Japanese language book

The Art of Skating, International Style
Madge and Edgar Syers
1913

Winter Sports in Switzerland
E.F. Benson
1913, focus on winter sports resorts in Switzerland

Figure Skating in the English Style
Humphry H. Cobb
1913, revised edition published in 1934, English Style focus

The Art of Skating
Irving Brokaw
1913, several editions

Uisu-sport

K. Pfeiffer, S. Facius
1914, Estonian language book

氷滑
Shirō Kawakubo
1915, Japanese language book

Hippodrome Skating Book: Practical Illustrations in the Art of Figure Skating
Charlotte Oelschlägel
1916

A Guide to Artistic Skating
George A. Meagher
1919

Konståkning på skridskor
Agard Palm
1919, Swedish language book

Skating: English, International, Speed
A.E. Crawley
1920

Skating With Bror Meyer
Bror Meyer
1921

Figure Skating for Women
James A. Cruikshank
1921

Skating and Bandy
Claude E. Benson, C.G. Tebbutt, Archibald Read, Arnold Tebbutt
1921, first published as part of the Badminton Library book on skating in 1892

Kunstlaufen auf dem Eise: zur Erlernung des Kunstschlittschuhfahrens mit einer kleinen Vorschule für Anfänger
S. Facius
1921, German language book

Der Eisläufer
Artur Vieregg
1921, German language book

スケート 1
Saburo Matsumiya
1921, Japanese language book

Ice King – General Skating Information
Julian T. Fitzgerald
1922

Figure Skating Simplified for Beginners
Major G. Baillie
1922, English Style focus

Kunst des Eislaufs: Praktische Winke
George Helfrich
1922, revised edition published 1924, German language book

Snow and Ice Sports: A Winter Manual
Elon Jessup
1923, one chapter on figure skating

Skøiteløpning
Yngvar Bryn
1924, Norwegian language book

Катание на коньках
Vladimir Abramovich Blyakh, M. Holoborodko
1924, Russian language book

Kunstfertigkeit im Eislaufen
Robert Holletschek, Erich Bartel, Max Schindler
1925, German language book (original version published in 1893)

Dancing on Ice: Described & Analyzed with Hints How To Do It
Ernest Law
1925, ice dance focus

Jazda figurowa na łyżwach
Jan Jankoswki
1925, Polish language book

Geschichte des Sports aller Völker und Zeiten
Gustav Adolf Erich Bogeng
1926, German language book

Theorie und Praxis des Kunstlaufes am Eise

Gilbert Fuchs
1926, German language book, revised in 1951

Фигурное катание на коньках
M.V. Khvostov
1926, Russian language book

Die Dame auf Schlittschuhen
George Helfrich
1926, women's skating focus, German language book

Letters To Young Winter Sportsmen
Brian Lunn
1927, chapters on various winter sports including figure skating

Eislaufschule
George Helfrich
1927, German language book

パニンのスケート
Shirō Kawakubo
1927, Japanese language book

Das Eissportbuch
Dr. Fritz Reuel
1928, German language book

... Фигурное катание на коньках
Nikolay Panin-Kolomenkin
1929, Russian language book

Winter Sports
Lord Lytton
1930, chapters on skating by Captain Duff-Taylor

Combined Figures and Ice-Valsing
Colonel H. Vaughan Kent
1930, English Style focus

Modern Figure Skating
T.D. Richardson
1930, revised edition published 1938

Hoe leer ik schoonrijden?: praktische wenken voor beginnende schoonrijders
J. Egmond, J.J. de Boer
1931, focuses on the basics of learning to skate, Dutch language book

The Elements of Figure Skating
Ernest Jones
1931, revised in 1951

Ice-Rink Skating: An Easy Way to Waltzing and the Bronze Medal
Sid G. Hedges
1932

Hiihto, luistelu, mäenlaskuja yhdistetyn mäenlaskun ja murtomaahiihdon säännöt
Workers' Sport Association
1932, Finnish language book

Patiner
Charles Sabouret, Paul Richer
1932, French language book

Nicholson on Figure Skating
Howard Nicholson
1933

Figure Skating Technique
Harold D.J. White
1933

Základy krasobruslení
Jaroslav Hainz
1933, Czech language book

スケートの手ほどきと競技を見る人の為に
Hideyo Koide
1933, Japanese language book

Vejledning i moderne Skøjteløb og Skøjtedans
Emmy Andersen
1934, Danish language book (later translated into French)

Das Kunstlaufen und der Tanz auf dem Eise
Gustav Feix
1935

The Beauty of Skating
Manfred Curry
1935

Die Schule des Eislaufes
O. Kaetterer
1935, German language book

Łyżwiarstwo
Jan Jankowski
1935, Polish language book

Eislauf: Kunst- und Schnellauf
Office of the "Reichssportführer"
1936, propaganda book promoting speed and figure skating at the 1936 Winter Olympics, German language book

Krasobruslení
Vladimir Koudelka
1936, revised edition published 1946, Czech language book

Ice Dances Published By Skating
U.S. Figure Skating Association
1936, three further editions published, the last being in 1948, ice dance focus

Skating
Captain Duff Taylor
1937

Ice Hockey, Skating and Dancing
Carl Ehrhardt
1937

Die Theorie der Eislaufsformen für den Anfänger und Fortgeschrittenen in vollendeter Form
Karl Nagele
1937, German language book

Mein Eiskunstlaufen im lebenden Bilde
Karl Schäfer
1937, German language book accompanied by 24 photo flipbooks illustrating various skating elements

Modern Skating
Frederic Lewis
1938

The Foundation of Skating: A Manual for Learners
Charles E. Salvesen
1938

Figure Skating as a Hobby
Diane Cummings
1938

Der Tanz auf dem Eise
Artur Vieregg
1938, ice dance focus

Champions All: Camera Studies by E.R. Hall
E.R. Hall, T.D. Richardson
1938, photo book

Ice-Rink Skating
T.D. Richardson

1938, revised edition published in 1949

Искусство катаня на коньках
Nikolay Panin-Kolomenkin
1938, Russian language book

Die Eisparade: Meisterinnen auf Schlittschuhen, wie sie sind und wie sie wurden: Kampf um den Weltmeisterthron
Hans Saalbach
1938, Though 90% biographical, does have chapters on skating in Austria, France and Japan, German language book

Skating (Barnes Dollar Sports Library)
Harold Putnam, Dwight Parkinson
1939

Kunstløps- ABC for liten og stor
Yngvar Bryn
1939, Norwegian language book

Ice Dancing
Monty Readhead
1939, revised edition published in 1968, ice dance focus

Maribel Y. Vinson's Advanced Figure Skating
Maribel Vinson Owen
1940

Figure Skating for Beginners with Illustrations from Moving Pictures

John S. MacLean
1940

How To Judge Figure Skating
Willy Böckl
1940, judging focus

Skridskoboken
Lars Grafström
1940, Swedish language book

Skridsko
Åke Blomqvist
1940, Swedish language book

Fundamentals of Figure Skating for the Beginner
Walter Arian
1941

Wintersportfibel, oder Die Kunst vergnüglich durch den Winter zu kommen
Luis Trenker, Carl J. Luther
1941, German language book

スケート年鑑 第1号(紀元2600 年-2601 年)
Japan Skating Federation
1941, Japanese language book

The Art of Plain Skating
Perry B. Rawson
1942

Le Patinage
Georges Larivière
1942, French language book

The Art of Skate Dancing
Perry B. Rawson
1943, ice and roller dance focus

Pairs Skating and Dancing on Ice
Rosemarie Stewart and Bob Dench
1943, pairs skating focus

The Sense in Sport
Howard Bass
1945, brief mention of tenice (tennis on ice) and Sonja Henie

Evaluation of Errors in Figures
Hank Beatty, U.S. Figure Skating Association
1945, revised editions published numerous times

Пързаляне с кънки: Състез. Правила
Venceslav Konstantinov Angelov, Ivan Panayotov
1946, Bulgarian language book

Skate Dance Shortcuts
Perry B. Rawson
1946, roller dance book that contains information pertinent to ice dance technique

Skate Dance Diagrams
Perry B. Rawson
1946, roller dance book that contains patterns for ice

dances

The Complete Figure Skater
T.D. Richardson
1948

Figure and Dance Skating
Paul von Gassner
1949, ice dance focus

Skøjtelob
Per Cock-Clausen
1950, Danish language book, revised version in 1964

Schule des Eislaufs
Artur Vieregg
1950, German language book

Skating On Ice: A Basis For Ice Dancing
Ivy Gale
1950, ice dance focus

Dancing on Ice
Erik van der Weyden
1950, ice dance focus

Łyżwiarstwo
Bolesław Staniszewski, Główny Komitet Kultury Fizycznej
1950, Polish language book

Lu Tingli
1951, Chinese language book

Bruslení
Běla Zachová, Jaroslav Zach
1951, Czech language book

Tance na ledě
Jaroslav Hainz, Miroslav Hasenöhrl
1951, Czech language book with ice dance focus

Championship Figure Skating: The Famous System of Gustave Lussi
Gustave Lussi, Maurice Richards
1951, instructional with a chapter on Dick Button

Skating With T.D. Richardson (later released as The Girls' Book of Skating)
T.D. Richardson
1952, revised editions in 1959 and 1964

Pravidla krasobruslení
Státním výborem pro tělesno výchovu a sport při vládě rep. Čs.
1953, Czech language book

Biologie der Körperübungen für Sportlehrer
Josef Nöcker
1953, German language book

フィギュア・スケート入門
Ryusuke Arisaka
1953, Japanese language book

Theorie und Praxis der Körperkultur
Helmut Haase
1954, German language book

Łyżwiarstwo dla młodzieży
Âkov Fedorovič Mel'nikov
1954, Polish language book

Eiskunstlauf von A bis Z: Technik, Organisation, Geschichte, Statistik. Ein Handbuch für Kunstläufer, Preisrichter, Vereinsfunktionäre, Sportlehrer und Freunde des Kunstlaufsports
Rudolf Kutzer
1955, German language book

スケーティング
Susumu Kobayashi
1955, Japanese language book

Eiskunstlaufen e. Einf
Dr. Freimut Stein
1955, nine further editions published, the latter being in 1975, German language book

Eistanzen; eine Einführung
Dr. Freimut Stein
1955, six further editions published, the latter being in 1965, German language book with an ice dance focus

Metodika krasobruslení
Josef Dědič, Vladislav Čáp

1956, Czech language book

Schijnwerpers op wintersporten: mensen in de sneeuw en op glad ijs
B. Baanen
1956, Dutch language winter sports book with a chapter on figure skating

ポピュラー・スケーティング やさしいスケートの入門書
Ryusuke Arisaka
1956, Japanese language book

Instructions to Young Skaters
Erik van der Weyden
1957

Łyżwiarstwo figurowe w szkolnym klubie sportowym
Anna Bursche-Lindnerowa
1957, Polish language book

Ръководство по кънки - спорт: Обикновено, бързо и фигурно пързаляне с кънки
Enyu St. Boyadzhiev
1958, Bulgarian language book

Eistanzen
Freimut Stein
1958, German language book

The Key to Rhythmic Ice Dancing
Muriel Kay
1958, revised edition published in 1992, ice dance focus

Základné korčuľovanie
H. Melková, M. Rovný
1958, Slovak language book

Know The Game: Skating, Ice & Roller
National Skating Association, Educational Productions Ltd.
1959

This Skating Age
Howard Bass
1959, Howard Bass

Wie lerne ich besser Schlittschuhlaufen? Teil I. Eislauf-Grundschule
Dr. Freimut Stein
1959, revised version in 1976, German language book

The Fun of Figure Skating: A Primer of the Art-Sport
Maribel Vinson Owen
1960

Krasobruslení pro rozhodčí a trenéry 1: Povinná jízda
Josef Dědič, Vladislav Čáp
1960, Czech language book

Het Ijstoerisme in Nederland: bepalingen voor het toerisme op de schaats in Nederland
Nederlandsche Schaatsenrijdersbond
1960, focuses mainly on touring (skating as tourism) but does reference figure skating, Dutch language book

Op de Schaats
H.J. Looman
1961, Dutch language book

Учитесь танцевать на коньках: Десять простых танцев на льду
Yuri Georgievich Nevsky
1961, Russian language book, ice dance focus

The Young Sportman's Guide to Ice Skating
Michael Kirby
1962

The Art of Figure Skating
T.D. Richardson
1962

Jeg løber på skøjter
Eva Meistrup
1962, Danish language book

Handleiding voor het wedstrijd-schaatsen en de training daarvoor
D. Havelaar
1962, Dutch language book

Auf eis geführt
Hans Behnke
1962, German language book

Фигурное катание на коньках: Сокр. пер. с англ.

Yakov Smushkin, I. Ershova
1962, Russian language book

Фигурное катание на коньках
Georgy Konstaninovich Felitsyn, L.P. Orlova, Union of Sports Societies and Organizations of the RSFSR
1962, Russian language book

Your Book of Skating
T.D. Richardson
1963

Skating For Everyone
Einar Jomland, Ron Priestley, James Waldo, Michael Kirby (ISIA)
1963

Krasobruslení pro rozhodčí a trenéry 2: Volná jízda jednotlivců
Josef Dědič, Miroslav Hasenöhrl
1963, Czech language book

Eislauf ABC
Dr. Freimut Stein, Karl Bedal
1963, six further editions published, the latter being in 1974, German language children's/young adult book

Instant Skating
Dick Button
1964

Figure Skating: Fun For Everyone

Canada Fitness and Amateur Sport Directorate, Melville Rogers
1964

Figure Skating for Beginners
Dennis L. Bird (under pseudonym John Noel)
1964

Učíme děti bruslit
Antonín Kaňka
1964, Czech language book

Uisutamine
Robert Kärsin, Harald Mähar, Vaike Paduri, F. Tross
1964, Estonian language book

How to Improve Your Skating
Einar Jomland, Ron Priestley, James Waldo, Michael Kirby (ISIA)
1965

Кънки за деца и юноши
Enyu St. Boyadzhiev
1965, Bulgarian language book

Veien til topps: moderne treningsmidler - programoppbygning: Skøyteløpernes treningsprogram
Stein Johnson
1965, Danish language book

フィギュアスケートたより 創刊号
Masamizu Kobayashi

1965, Japanese language book

スケート入門―早く上達する秘訣
Susumu Kobayashi
1965, Japanese language book

Grunnskole: kunstløp
Per A. Jansen, Norges Skøyteforbund
1965, Norwegian skating book

Skating For Everyone
Arthur N. Foxe
1966

Le Patinage: Sport d'Elite
Raymonde du Bief
1966, French language book

Eiskunstlaufen eine Einführung
Freimut Stein
1966, German language book

Ice Dances: Figures & Exercises
U.S. Figure Skating Association
1966, ice dance focus

Фигурное катание на коньках: Наглядное учеб. пособие
D.D. Donskoy, Yuri Georgievich Nevsky
1966, Russian language book

Eislauf im Bild

Manfred Schnelldorfer, Wolfgang Roucka
1967, German language book

Łyżwiarstwo: metodyka nauczania, technika, historia
Włodzimierz Starosta
1967, Polish language book

Искусство фигурного катания на коньках: Учеб.-метод. пособие
Yakov Smushkin
1967, Russian language book

Ice Skating
Peri Horne
1968

Winter Sports
Howard Bass
1968

Traumnote 6 für Emmi Danzer: hinter den Kulissen des Eiskunstlaufs
Heinz Prüller
1968, German language book

Basic Ice Skating Skills: An Official Handbook Prepared for the United States Figure Skating Association
Robert S. Ogilvie, U.S. Figure Skating Association
1968, revised editions published numerous times

Drsanje
Jože Biber, Solski center za telesno vzgojo
1968, Slovenian language book

Figure Skating
Marion Proctor
1969

Schaatsen
Frans Ensink
1969, Dutch language book

Азбука начинающего фигуриста- Читайте подробнее на
Samson Glazer
1969, Russian language book

Britt Elfvings konståkningsskola
Britt Elfving, Svenska konståkningsförbundet
1969, Swedish language book

Konståkning: träningsråd för nybörjare
Bengt G. Lago
1969, Swedish language book

Konståkning: Den Moderna Handboken
Mona Lisa Eglund-Crispin
1969, Swedish language book

Success in Ice Skating
Howard Bass
1970

В рамке катка: Фигурное катание: каким его видят тренер и журналист

Elena Chaikovskaya, Lyudmila Nikolaevna Dobrova
1970, Russian language book

International Encyclopaedia of Winter Sports
Howard Bass
1971

ABC vor der Schaatsport
Piet Bergström
1971, covers both speed and figure skating, instructional with short biographies of Dutch skaters, Dutch language book

...и серебряный иней...
Stanislav Zhuk
1971, Russian language book

Krasobruslení: povinná a volná jízda jednotlivců
Josef Dědič, Jaroslav Hainz
1972, Czech language book

Základné korčuľovanie a hry na ľade
Ladislav Horský
1972, Slovak language book

Edges
Roger F. Turner
1973

I Can Teach You To Figure Skate
Tina Noyes
1973

Ice Skating: Form, Fitness and Speed
D. Phillips
1974

Complete Beginner's Guide to Ice Skating
Edward F. Dolan
1974

Figure Skating
Ellen Burka
1974

Off-Ice Training for Figure Skaters
Tudor Bompa
1974

Uisutamise õpetamine
Mai Männiste
1974, Estonian language book

Oppelt Standard Method of Therapeutic & Recreational Ice Skating
Kurt Oppelt
1974, focus on working with Special Olympic skaters

Patinage et danse sur glace: technique, entraînement, compétition
Michel Delore
1974, French language book

Eiskunstlauf für Fortgeschrittene
Erich Zeller

1975, German language book

Фигурное катание на коньках: Учебник для ин-тов физ. Культур
R.A. Asoskov, V.A. Vyunik
1975, Russian language book

Фигурное катание
Elena Chaikovskaya
1975, Russian language book

Ледовая сюита
Viktor Ryzhkin
1975, Russian language book

Better Ice Skating for Boys and Girls
George Sullivan
1976

Better Ice Skating
Richard Arnold
1976

Patinage
Alain Billouin, Philippe Pélissier
1976

Světové piruety
Josef Dědič
1976, Czech language book

Ice Dancing: A Manual for Judges and Skaters

Sidney V. Soanes
1976, ice dance focus

Фигурное катание для всех
Alexei Mishin
1976, Russian language book

The Technique of Skating
Jacques Gerschwiler, Otto Hügin
1977

Előbb a szárazon, azután a jégen: A korcsolyázás alapjai
Alice Peters, Zoltán Szijj
1977, Hungarian language book

Metodyka nauczania i technika łyżwiarstwa (łyżwiarstwo podstawowe z elementami łyżwiarstwa figurowego i szybkiego oraz hokeja) – Volumes 1& 2
Włodzimierz Starosta, Zbigniew Osiński
1977, Polish language book

The Skater's Manual
Kenny Isely
1978

Enjoying Skating
Diagram Group
1978

Step By Step Ice Skating Guide
Carol Butterworth
1978

Inside Ice Skating
Einar Jonland, Jim Fitzgerald
1978

Let's Go Skating
Howard Bass
1978

Figure Skating
Dianne de Leeuw, Steve Lehrman
1978

最新フィギュア・スケート技術百科　ヨゼフ・デェディッチ
Kazuo Ohashi, Tadahiro Goto
1978, Japanese language translation of "Krasobruslení" by Josef Dědič

Фигурное катание на коньках- Читайте подробнее на
Alexander Gandelsman
1978, Russian language book

Ice Skating for Everybody: Your Self-Teaching Guide
Peter Dunfield, Irwin J. Polk
1978

Konståkning för ungdom
Jane Sörman
1978, Swedish language book

Ice Skating Made Easy
Richard Arnold

1979

New York Times Encyclopedia Of Sports, Volume 9: Winter Sports
Gene Brown
1979

The Illustrated Encyclopedia of Ice Skating
Mark Heller
1979

Skating For Pleasure
Howard Bass
1979

Фигурно пързаляне: Учебник-записки
Maria G. Georcheva
1979, Bulgarian language book (revised edition released in 1983)

Richtig eislaufen
Monika Maier
1979, German language book

Sport und Spiel auf dem Eis: Eisschnellauf, Eiskunstlauf, Eishockey, Bandy, Curling, Eisschiessen, Eissegeln
Heinz Polednik
1979, German language book

Origins of Ice Dance Music
Muriel Kay

1979, ice dance focus
Sporty zimowe. Cz. 1, Łyżwiarstwo
Barbara Czyżewska
1979, Polish language book

Школа в фигурном катании
Alexei Mishin
1979, Russian language book

Фигурное катание на коньках: Основы техники одиноч. произвол. катания на коньках: Лекция для студентов-заочников
Lyudmila Ivanovna Kubashevskaya
1979, Russian language book

Фигурное катание на коньках: Методика обучения обяз
Irina Vasilievna Absalyamova
1979, Russian language book, focus on compulsory figures

Figure Skating with Carlo Fassi
Carlo Fassi
1980

Skating: Elegance on Ice
Howard Bass
1980

The Love of Skating
Howard Bass
1980

Ice Skating
Howard Bass
1980

Фигурно пързаляне за деца и юноши
Ivan Georgiev Ivanov
1980, Bulgarian language book

Ice Skating Is For Me
Lowell A. Dickmeyer
1980, children's/young adult book

Choreography & Style For Ice Skaters
Ricky Harris
1980, choreography focus

Ice Dancing Illustrated
Lorna Dyer
1980, ice dance focus

Innføring i kunstløp
Bjørg Ellen Ringdal
1980, Norwegian skating book

Creative Ice Skating: Ice Dancing, Freestyle and Pair Skating
Frances Dorsey, Wendy Williams
1980

Шесть баллов
Elena Chaikovskaya

1980, Russian language book

Хореография и фигурное катание
Lyudmila Pakhomova
1980, Russian language book, focus on choreography

Happier Figure Skating Handbook
Patricia Jackson, South African Ice Skating Association
1981

The Easy Ice Skating Book
Jonah Kalb
1981

Конькобежный спорт
G.M. Panov, B.P. Baryshev
1981, Azerbaijani language book

Uisutamaõpetamine
Mai Männiste
1981, Estonian language book

Patinage idéologique
René Lourau
1981, French language book

Фигурное катание: коммент. к судейству
Elena Vasilievna Absalyamova, Evgenia Bogdanova
1981, Russian language book

Konståkning: modellinlärning
Mona Bodin, Elisabet Poulsen, Lars-Eric Uneståhl

1981, Swedish language book

冬のスポーツ
Sapporo City Board of Education
1981, two chapters on figure skating written by Ryusuke Arisaka, Japanese language book

The Ice Skater's Bible
Richard Stephenson, Theodore G. Clarke
1982

How To Succeed at Skating
Monika Baier
1982

Better Sport Skating: The Key to Improved Performance
Richard Arnold
1982

Sportovní příprava III. Bruslení a základy krasobruslení
Jana Mayerová
1982, Czech language book

Choreographie und Eiskunstlauf
Deutsche Hochschule für Körperkultur Leipzig
1982, German language book, focus on choreography

Korcsolyázás
László Jakabházy
1982, Hungarian language book

Ice Skating Fundamentals
Marilyn G. House
1983

Skating
Boy Scouts of America
1983, children's/young adult book

溜冰溜冰
Chen Ji
1983, Chinese language book

The Batchelors: Figure Skating Manual
Vera, Eric and Erica Batchelor, South African Ice Skating Association
1984

Skater's Handbook
John 'Misha' Petkevich
1984

Ice Skating Basics
Norman MacLean
1984

The BBC Book of Skating
Sandra Stevenson
1984

Skateaway (A Channel Four Book)
Robin Cousins
1984, children's/young adult book

Krasobruslení pro trenéry 3: a 2. třídy
František Blaták
1984, Czech language book

フィギュアスケート
Kuniko Nakamura
1984, Japanese language book

The Parent's Guide to Competitive Figure Skating: How to Start Your Child on the Way to the Top
Robert S. Ogilvie
1985

Skateology
Sidney Broadbent
1985

Metodika, technika a organizace základního bruslení
Dagmar Havránková
1985, Czech language book

Dancing On Skates
Richard Arnold
1985, ice dance focus

基本レッスン スケート
Kazuo Ohashi
1985, Japanese language book

フィギュアスケート入門
Nobuo Sato

1985, Japanese language book

Cub Scout Sports: Skating
Boy Scouts of America
1986, children's/young adult book

Figure It Out: Think Your Way to Skating Great Figures
Nina Stark-Slapnik
1986, focus on compulsory figures

Eislauf, Eiskunstlauf, Eisschnellauf: Literatur
Sepp Schönmetzler, Thomas Moser
1986, German language book

Praxis und Theorie des österreichischen
Eiskunstlaufsports: Sanierungsvorschläge - ein
Bundesleistungszentrum für Eiskunstlauf
Claudia Kristofics-Binder
1986, German language book

Let's Go Ice Skating
Richard Arnold
1987

Figure Skating
Margaret Ryan
1987, children's/young adult book

花□ 溜冰
Wang Shuben
1987, Chinese language book

Pair Skating as Sport and Art
Tamara Moskvina
1987, pairs skating focus

Sports Illustrated Figure Skating: Championship Techniques
John 'Misha' Petkevich
1988

Super Book of Ice Skating
Howard Bass
1988

Ice Show Manual
Canadian Figure Skating Association
1988, focus on organizing club carnivals

Eiskunstlaufen mit Denise Biellmann: ein Lehrbuch für alle; Anfang, Figuren, Doppelsprünge, Pirouetten, Bewertung, Eistanzen
Otto Hügin
1988, German language book

Korčuľovanie a ľadový hokej
Jaroslav Starší
1988, Slovak language book

Ice Dancing Made Easy
Theodore Clarke
1989, ice dance focus

Ice Skating

Tim Wood
1990

Skating
Donna Bailey
1990

Конькобежный спорт
Boris Andrianovich Stenin
1990, Azerbaijani language book

Фигурно пързаляне: Уч. помагало за специалисти
Lahezar Zahariev
1990, Bulgarian language book

溜冰学 技巧
Dingita
1990, Chinese language book

Muodostelmaluistelun ohjaajan opas
Suomen taitoluisteluliitto
1990, Finnish language book, focus on coaching

Biofeedback-Methoden zur Leistungssteigerung im Sport: Beispiele aus der Praxis in den Sportarten Sportschießen, Badminton und Eiskunstlauf
Christine Hufnagl
1990, German language book

Eiskunstlauf: Trainingsaspekte und psychologische Grundlagen
Sabine Paal

1990, German language sports psychology book geared towards skaters

Фигурное катание на коньках : Страницы отеч. истории : Буклет
R.A. Chubrik
1990, Russian language book

Фигурное катание на коньках: Пособие для учителя
Mikhail Ivanovich Vorobyov, Irina Mikhailovna Medvedeva
1990, Russian language book, focus on coaching

Let's Go Skating
Alex Taylor
1991

Le Patinage Artistique
Didier Gailhaguet
1991, French language book

The Complete Manual of Compulsory Dances
Jeff R. Lerner
1992, ice dance focus

Håndbok: Figure skating
Lillehammer Olympic Organizing Committee
1992, Norwegian language book

Крылатые коньки- Читайте подробнее
А.А. Shelukhin
1992, Russian language book

Figure Skating: A Practical Guide for the Beginner
Skater, The Aussie Skater
National Ice Skating Association of Australia
1993

Handbook of New Era Figures
Robert S. Ogilvie
1993, focus on compulsory figures

Get The Edge: Sport Psychology for Figure Skaters
Shawna L. Palmer
1993, sports psychology book geared towards skaters

Aussie Skate Program: Learn to Skate the NISAA Way
National Ice Skating Association of Australia
1994

Parent's Guide to Test and Competitive Skating
Canadian Figure Skating Association
1994

Figure Skating: A Celebration
Beverley Smith
1994

Super Skaters: World Figure Skating Stars
Steve Milton
1994, children's/young adult book

Patterns of Russian Ice Dance
Elena Chaikovskaya
1994, ice dance focus

The Complete Manual of Compulsory Ice Dances
Jeff R. Lerner
1994, ice dance focus

Базовые движения в фигурном катании на коньках и методика обучения им
Cvetanka Aleksandrova Stefanova
1994, Russian language book

Ice Skating: Steps to Success
Karin Künzle-Watson, Stephen J. DeArmond
1995

Women on Ice: Feminist Responses to the Tonya Harding/Nancy Kerrigan Spectacle
Cynthia Baughman
1995

Figure Skating: Sharpen Your Skills
Patricia Hagen
1995

Little Girls in Pretty Boxes: The Making and Breaking of Gymnasts and Figure Skaters
Joan Ryan
1995

Secrets of the Soviet Skaters: Off-Ice Training Methods
Tamara Moskvina
1995

Skøjteløb, gymnastik og sport: om at forstå betydningen

for kvinder.
Else Trangbæk
1995, Danish language book

Skater's Edge Sourcebook: Ice Skating Resource Guide
Alice Berman
1995, directory

Muodostelmaluistelu: opas ohjaajille ja opettajille
Anu Jääskeläinen
1995, Finnish language book, focus on coaching

Passion patinage: des origines à nos jours
Jean-Christophe Berlot
1995, French language book

A Year in Figure Skating
Beverley Smith
1996

A Passion To Skate: An Intimate View of Figure Skating
Sandra Bezic, David Hayes
1996

Skate: 100 Years Of Figure Skating
Steve Milton, Barbara McCutcheon
1996

Superstars on Ice: Figure Skating Champions
Patty Cranston
1996, children's/young adult book

Témoignage de Laurent Depouilly, Entraîneur National de Patinage Artistique
Laurent Depouilly
1996, French language book

Figure Skating For Dummies
Kristi Yamaguchi, Christy Ness, Jody Beachem
1997

Figure Skating School: A Professionally Structured Course from Basic Steps to Advanced Techniques
Peter Morrissey
1997

Talking Figure Skating: Behind The Scenes in the World's Most Glamourous Sport
Beverley Smith
1997

Secrets of Skating
Oksana Baiul
1997

Skating Dreams: The Official Scrapbook Of The United States Figure Skating Association
U.S. Figure Skating Association
1998

Skate Talk: Figure Skating In The Words Of The Stars
Steve Milton
1998

The Official Book of Figure Skating
Mary Tiegreen, ABC Sports, U.S. Figure Skating Association
1998

Magic on Ice: Figure Skating Stars, Tips and Facts
Patty Cranston h
1998, children's/young adult book

Pienin askelin luistelutaitoon
Timo Salovita, Merja Autio-Kokko
1998, Finnish language book

五十嵐文男の華麗なるフィギュアスケート
Fumio Igarashi
1998, Japanese language book

Le Patinage Artistique: Saison 1999
Jean-Christophe Berlot
1999, French language book

The Essential Figure Skater
Bernie and Nikki Schallehn, Patti Tashman
2000

誰も語らなかった 知って感じるフィギュアスケート観戦術
Shizuka Arakawa
2000

Inside Figure Skating
Alina Sivorinovsky
2000

Spinning into the Spotlight: Figure Skating in Saskatchewan, 1883-1996
Sandra Bingaman, Saskatchewan Section, CFSA
2000

幼儿溜冰教学
Xu Hui
2001, Chinese language book, focus on coaching

Les Stars du Patinage
Nelson Monfort
2001, French language book

The Complete Book of Figure Skating
Carole Shulman
2002

Les Riches Heures Du Patinage
Jean-Christophe Berlot
2002, French language book

The Second Mark: Courage, Corruption, and the Battle for Olympic Gold
Joy Goodwin
2003

Frozen Assets: The New Order Of Figure Skating
Mark A. Lund
2003

Figure Skating Now: Olympic and World Stars

Gérard Châtaigneau, Steve Milton
2003

Tähtiä jäällä: tarinoita taitoluistelusta
Anu Puromies, Suomen taitoluisteluliitto
2003, Finnish language book

Terminologievergleich Eiskunstlaufen Deutsch - Italienisch - Englisch: Schwerpunkt Einzellauf
Eva Thurnher
2003, German language book

Eiskunstlauf in Österreich: eine Analyse aus der Sicht von SportlerInnen und Eltern
Anni Luftensteiner
2003, German language book

Winter Sports Medicine: Handbook
James L. Moeller, Sami F. Rifat
2004, focus on sports medicine

Tipps für Eiskunstlauf
Waltraud Witte
2004, German language book

Eislaufen leichter und sicher erlernbar: ein Lehrbuch für Alle
Otto Hügin
2004, German language book

Physiologisches Belastungs-Beanspruchungsprofil und sportmotorische Leistungsfähigkeit im Eiskunstlauf

Irene K. Fuchs
2004, German language book

Eiskunstlauf - Eishockey - Eisschnelllauf: ein terminologischer Vergleich Französisch - Deutsch – Französisch
Sigrid Pichler
2004, German language book

On Edge: Backroom Dealing, Cocktail Scheming, Triple Axels, and How Top Skaters Get Screwed
Jon Jackson
2005

A Spectator's Guide to Figure Skating
Debbi Wilkes
2005

Le patinage artistique: une certaine vision de l'acrobatie
Denise Neanne
2005, French language book

Eissportarten: Eisschnelllauf, Eiskunstlauf und Eishockey der Universiade 2005 ; ein terminologischer Vergleich, Deutsch – Italienisch
Bruno Bassi
2005, German language book

Kunstmusik in Eiskunstlauf, Synchronschwimmen und rhythmischer Gymnastik von 1990 bis zur Gegenwart
Johanna Beisteiner
2005, German language book

Eiskunstlauf: Glossar Deutsch – Russisch
Claudia Schleret
2005, German language book

氷上のアーティストたち: 日本フィギュアスケートトリノを目指す銀盤の選手たち
Junko Yaginuma
2005, Japanese language book

君なら翔べる!
Nobuo and Kumiko Sato
2005, Japanese language book

Inside the Olympics: A Behind-the-Scenes Look at the Politics, the Scandals and the Glory of the Games
Dick Pound
2006

Krasobruslení: škola bruslení, choreografie, pravidla, vybavení, trénink
Gabriela Žilková Hrázská
2006, Czech language book

愛するスケートに何が起こったのか?: 女子フィギュア・トリノ選考の真実
Emi Watanabe
2006, Japanese language book

Fundamentals of Alignment & Classical Alignment for Figure Skaters
Annette T. Thomas

2006, focus on ballet for figure skaters

女子フィギュアスケート: 氷上に描く物語
Junko Yaginuma
2006, Japanese language book, women's focus

Eiskunstlaufen als Breitensport: Erstellung und Erprobung eines Programms zur Vermittlung von Grundfertigkeiten im Bereich der Erwachsenen
Hanna Opitz
2007, German language book

Wonders on Ice: Figure Skating in Minnesota
Moira F. Harris
2007

Magije umetničkog klizanja
Dobrila Knežević
2007, Serbian language book

Figure Skating's Greatest Stars
Steve Milton
2009

Eiskunstlauf Basics
Waltraud Witte
2009, German language book

フィギュアスケートを100倍楽しく見る方法
Shizuka Arakawa
2009, Japanese language book

Самоучитель по фигурному катанию- Читайте подробнее на
N. Kurbanov
2009, Russian language book

Фигурное катание: только звезды: международные турниры: эксклюзивный фотоальбом
Alexander Wilf, Elena Vaytsekhovskaya
2009, Russian language photo book

Educación para la salud practica el patinaje
Alejandro Morales Negrillo
2009, Spanish language book

Taking The Ice: Success Stories from the World of Canadian Figure Skating
PJ Kwong
2010

Spin It Figure Skating
Paul C. Challen
2010, children's/young adult book

Figure Skating
Joseph Alan Gustaitis
2010, children's/young adult book

Taitoluistelun lumo
Leena Lehtolainen, Kaisa Viitanen
2010, Finnish language book

Chemnitz Eissterne
Martina Martin
2010, German language book

Triumph on Ice: The New World of Figure Skating
Jean Riley Senft
2011

5歳の寺子屋 乗り越える力
Shizuka Arakawa
2011, Japanese language book

Lessons in Classic Ballet for the Figure Skater
Annette T. Thomas
2011, focus on ballet for skaters

フィギュアスケート 美のテクニック
Mie Noguchi, Yutaka Higuchi
2011, Japanese language book

Zagrebačke pahuljice i sinkro-svijet
Zoran Kovačević
2012, Croatian language book, focus on synchro skating

アイスモデリスト
Junko Yaginuma
2012, Japanese language book

Push Dick's Button: A Conversation Of Skating From A Good Part Of The Last Century - And A Little Tomfoolery
Dick Button

2013

Skating To Sochi
Beverley Smith
2013

こころのホットミルク
Chisato Shiina
2013, Japanese language book

トップスケーターの流儀 中野友加里が聞く9人のリアルストーリー
Yukari Nakano
2013, Japanese language book

Sur neige et sur glace: sports d'hiver: fiches thématiques sport et handicap
Stefan Häusermann, Reini Linder
2015, French language book, focus on working with Special Olympic skaters

プロのフィギュア観戦術
Akiko Suzuki
2015, Japanese language book

Фигурное катание: от голландского шага - до "двойного тулупа": учебное пособие
Anatoly Petrovich Mironov
2015, Russian language book

Фигурное катание как космический полет
Alexei Mishin, Victor Shapiro
2015, Russian language book

Artistry on Ice: Figure Skating Skills and Style
Nancy Kerrigan, Mary Spencer
2016

Jään lumo
Leena Lehtolainen, Kaisa Viitanen, Tammi Kustannusosakeyhtiö
2016, Finnish language book

フィギュアスケート ジャンプ完全レッスン 動画で技術と魅せ方に差がつく－コツがわかる本！－
Yukari Nakano
2017, Japanese language book

トップスケーターのすごさがわかるフィギュアスケート
Yukari Nakano
2017, Japanese language book

Figure Skating Explained: A Spectator's Guide to Competitive Figure Skating
S.J. Thomas
2018

현대) 피겨 스케이트 교본 : 환상의 스케이트
Hyundai Leisure Research Society
2018, Korean language book

Patterns on the Black Ice: The Art & Sport of Figure Skating
Louise Vacca Dawe
2019, focus on compulsory figures

Starke Seiten – Wintersport
Egon Theiner, Trixi Schuba, Jens Weißflog, Eva Walkner, Marcel Hirschner, Mario Stecher
2019, German language book

Why Black and Brown Kids Don't Ice Skate
Joel Savary
2020, focus on black and brown skaters

Ma fille (mon fils) ne le sait pas encore mais le patinage est un sport très glissant: petit guide à l'intention des parents
Eric and Soonmi Lehmann
2020, French language book, guide for parents of skaters

Фигурное катание: Стальные девочки
Elena Vaytsekhovskaya
2020, Russian language book

L'arabesque: du patinage artistique à la médecine: journal d'une athlète de haut niveau
Soonmi Lehmann
2021, French language book

フィギュアスケート スピン完全レッスン 動画で技術と魅せ方に差がつく－コツがわかる本－
Yukari Nakano
2021, Japanese language book

Фигурно пързаляне: Учебник-записки
Tatjana Dimčeva Jordanova

2022, Bulgarian language book

Figure Skating: Guide to Figure Skating for Complete Beginners
Michelle Trejo
2022

Winning Spirit Figure Skating: Find Your Inner Game
Tom Mitchell
2022, focus on sports psychology

A Constraints-led Approach to Figure Skating Coaching
Garrett Lucash
2022, focus on coaching

A Different Kind of Edge: Transitioning from Skater to Coach: A Guide to Figure Skating Foundations
Jessica Rensch
2022

SKATING HISTORY

When Frederick William Foster published the first bibliography of skating in 1898, he wrote, ""A history of skating as a whole has yet to written. Most extant writing on the general history of skating contains almost as much myth and false suggestion as truth."

We've come a long way since 1898, baby! Though you'll find a ton of fascinating skating history in the general books listed above, these offerings focusing entirely on *the sport's history will knock your skates off.*

While you're at, check it Skate Guard blog at http://skateguard1.blogspot.ca. There are hundreds of fascinating and fabulous articles on the sport's history available 24/7, free of charge.

A History of the National Skating Association of Great Britain, 1879-1901 with a Catalogue of the Exhibition of Skates and Skating Matters in 1902
National Skating Association (Edgar Syers, John Moyer Heathcote, Montagu Sneade Monier-Williams, Dr. George Herbert Fowler, Henry Ellington)
1902

The Skater's Cavalcade: Fifty Years of Skating
A.C.A. Wade
1939

The First Twenty-Five Years of the United States Figure Skating Association, 1921-1946
U.S. Figure Skating Association
1946

An Approved History of The Olympic Games
William M. Henry
1948

Five Thousand Years of Winter-Sports
Mario Cereghini
1955

Ice Skating

T.D. Richardson
1956

The Ancient Art of Skating
Robert L. Merriam
1957, hand-written

Skaters of The Fens
Alan Bloom
1958

Ice-Skating: A History
Nigel Brown
1959

Jégországból jelentkezem - Színes Sportkönyvtár
Vitray Tamás, Dr. Elemér Terták
1963, Hungarian language book

Encyclopedia of the Olympic Winter Games
Erich Kamper
1964

Konståkningens 100-åriga historia: utveckling, OS-VM-referater, intervjuer och berättelser
Gunnar Bang
1966, Swedish language book

Schaatsen
S.C.A. Tan
1967, Dutch language book

The Olympic Games
International Skating Union
1968

Le Patinage sur Glace: Historique
Jeanine Hagnauer
1968, French language book

Seventy-Five Years of European and World's
Championships in Figure Skating
International Skating Union
1970, historical competition results

Both Feet On The Ground: The Story of a Family
Firm...
Stubbs & Burt Ltd.
1971, skate making

American Women in Sports
Phyllis Hollander
1972

Wonderful World of Skates: Seventeen Centuries of
Skating
Arthur M. Goodfellow
1972

日本スケート史
Japan Skating History Publishing Association
1975, Japanese language book

Ирина Роднина

Anatoly Tchaikovsky
1977, Russian language book

The Big Red Machine: The Rise and Fall of Soviet Olympic Champions
Yuri Brokin
1977, Soviet skating history

Reader's Guide to Figure Skating's Hall of Fame
Benjamin T. Wright, Gregory R. Smith, U.S. Figure Skating Association
1978

The American Skating Mania: Ice Skating in the Nineteenth Century
Luna Lambert, Smithsonian Institute
1979

Our Skating Heritage
Dennis L. Bird
1979

The Ice Skating Book
Robert Sheffield, Richard Woodward
1980

The Skating Scene: Champions & Championships, The Fact Book of Skating
Arthur R. Goodfellow
1981

日本のスケート発達史：スピード・フィギュア・アイスホッケー

Japan Skating Federation
1981, Japanese language book

The Golden Age of Canadian Figure Skating
David Young
1984

Nekonečné stopy bruslí
Jarmila Šastná-Königová
1985, Czech language book

Winteraerdigheden, winternaerigheden: beknopt
overzicht van het ijsvermaak en de geschiedenis van de
schaats
René Dijkstra
1985, Dutch language book

New Zealand Ice Skating Association Inc.: 50th Jubilee,
1937-1987, History of the N.Z.I.S.A. Inc.
Rhona Whitehouse, New Zealand Ice Skating
Association
1987

The Fine Art Of Figure Skating: An Illustrated History
And Portfolio Of Stars
Julia Whedon
1988

Schaatsen en schaatsenmakers in de 19e en 20e eeuw
A.C. Broere
1988, Dutch language book, focus on antique skates

Klizanje u Zagrebu
Horvatić
1991, Croatian language book

ISU Office Holders Through The Years and ISU
Congresses 1892-1990: Chronological Lists Compiled
from the Minutes of ISU Congresses and ISU
Communications
James Koch, Benjamin T. Wright, International Skating
Union
1992

Results 1968-1991: Figure Skating Championships
Benjamin T. Wright, International Skating Union
1992

Skating Around the World: International Skating Union,
The One Hundredth Anniversary History 1892-1992
Benjamin T. Wright, International Skating Union
1992

Figure Skating: The Evolution of Dance on Ice
Lynn Copley-Graves
1992, ice dance focus

Sølv var nederlag: Norges skøyteforbund 100 år: 1893-1993
Per Hauge-Moe, Norges skøyteforbund
1992, Norwegian language book

Canadian Figure Skating Association 1887-1990,
Reflections on the CFSA

Teresa Moore, Canadian Figure Skating Association
1993

Skating In America (1921-1996): The 75th Anniversary History of the United States Figure Skating Association
Benjamin T. Wright, U.S. Figure Skating Association
1996

Van glis tot klapschaats: schaatsen en schaatsenmakers in Nederland, 1200 tot heden
Wiebe Blauw
2001, Dutch language book, focus on antique skates

Łyżwiarski Jubileusz: Polski Związek Łyżwiarstwa Szybkiego: 80 lat
Jacek Żemantowski, Kazimierza Kowalczyka, Leszka Ułasiewicza
2001, Polish language book

La historia del patinaje artistico
Anastasia Suen
2003, Spanish language book, children's/young adult book

Cracked Ice: Figure Skating's Inner World
Sonia Bianchetti Garbato
2004, historical information on the ISU and judging

日本スケート連盟75年のあゆみ
Japan Skating Federation
2004, Japanese language book

Figure Skating: A History
James R. Hines
2006

Фигурное катание в России: факты, события, судьбы
Alexei Mishin, Yuri Yakymchuk
2007, Russian language book

The English Style: Figure Skating's Oldest Tradition
James R. Hines
2008, English Style focus

Frozen in Time: The Enduring Legacy of the 1961 U.S. Figure Skating Team
Nikki Nichols
2008, focus on the 1961 Sabena Crash

Indelible Tracings: The Story of the 1961 U.S. World Figure Skating Team
Patricia Shelley Bushman
2010, focus on the 1961 Sabena Crash

Historical Dictionary of Figure Skating
James R. Hines
2011

Indelible Images: An Illustrated History Of The 1961 U.S. World Figure Skating Team
Patricia Shelley Bushman
2011, focus on the 1961 Sabena Crash

Acht eeuwen schaatsen in en om Amsterdam

Niko Mulder, Jos Pronk, Nelly Moerman
2014, Dutch language book

Serge Gilbert et le patinage artistique à Québec
Serge Gilbert
2014, French language book

A tél bajnokai: fejezetek a magyar műkorcsolyázás történetéből: jégen írt sportsikerek Zuglóban
Máté Millisits, Lajos Szabó, Hungarian Olympic and Sports Museum
2014, Hungarian language book

Белые игры под грифом "секретно": СССР и зимние Олимпийские игры 1956-1988: историко-документальная выставка
N.G. Tomalina, I.V. Kazarina, M.I. Prozumenschchikov, N.V. Pereresudina, S.V. Borak
2014, Russian language book

Figure Skating in the Formative Years: Singles, Pairs, and the Expanding Role of Women
James R. Hines
2015

Piruetem przez historię
Bogdan Chruścicki, Jacek Żemantowski
2015, Polish language book

Lace Up: A History of Skates in Canada
Jean-Marie Leduc, Sean Graham, Julie Léger
2017, focus on antique skates

Figure Skating Competition Handbook: Who Won What at All the Major Competitions From 1891 to Present Day
Greg Fox
2017, historical competition results

Skates Made of Bone: A History
Beverly A. Thurber
2020, focus on antique skates

The Almanac of Canadian Figure Skating
Ryan Stevens
2022, revised edition published in 2023, focus on Canadian figure skating history

Příběhy našeho krasobruslení
Alice Lily Neradová
2022, Czech language book

End of the Compulsories: A Remembrance
James R. Hines
2022, focus on compulsory figures and compulsory dances

Technical Merit: A History of Figure Skating Jumps
Ryan Stevens, foreword by Donald Jackson
2023

SHOWS AND TOURS

Over the years, touring ice shows like Ice Capades, Ice Follies, Holiday on Ice and Disney on Ice have captivated audiences and inspired many people to take to the ice for the first time. These books recount the compelling stories of ice shows and pantomimes and touring ice revues.

Earl's Court
Claude Langdon
1953

Glorious Wembley
Howard Bass
1982

Die Wiener Eisrevue. Ein verklungener Traum
Dr. Roman Seeliger
1993, German language book

Holiday on Ice: The First Fifty Years
Ted Shuffle
1994

Stars On Ice: An Intimate Look At Skating's Greatest Tour
Barry Wilner
1998

EisballettRatte: die abenteuerliche Karriere der jungen Artistin
Jackie Batallier-Rhyner
2002, German language book

Admiralspalast: Die Geschichte eines Berliner
Jost Lehne
2006, German language book

Die Wiener Eisrevue Einst Botschafterin Österreichs -
heute Legende
Dr. Roman Seeliger
2008, German and English language book

Holiday on Ice: Magic Moments
Edel Germany GmbH, Holiday on Ice
2009, German language coffee table photography book

Memories of the Great American Ice Shows
Jimmy Lawrence
2012

Traumfabrik auf dem Eis. Von der Wiener Eisrevue zu
Holiday on Ice
Bernhard Hachleitner, Isabelle Lechner
2014, German language book

The Magical Life of an Ice Folliette: A Shipstads and
Johnson Ice Follies Memoir
Marlene Birrel Beckman
2020

Catherine Littlefield: A Life In Dance
Sharon Skeel
2020, biography with historical information on the ice
shows at the Centre Theatre in New York

To Be A Soldier: Military Memoirs 1927-1960
Ivers and Karen Worley Funk
2021, chapter on the ice shows at the Casa Carioca nightclub in Germany

SKATING CLUBS AND RINKS

Not only have skating clubs and rinks been skater's homes away from home for centuries, they have borne witness to important changes in the sport. These books explore the stories of some of the places behind the sport's people.

The Figure Skating Tests of the Cambridge Skating Club
Cambridge Skating Club
1900

Chronik des Wiener Eislaufvereines
Franz Biberhofer
1906, German language book

Eisbahnen und Eislaufvereine: Anleitung zur Anlegung und Unterhaltung von Eisbahnen, Gründung und Verwaltung von Eislaufvereinen u.s.w.
George Helfrich
1907, German language book, guide to managing rinks and skating clubs

Cottage-Eislauf-Verein in Wien

V. Bresnik
1909, German language book

Berättelse över Stockholms allmänna skridskoklubbs
verksamhet 1883-1923
August Anderberg, Victor Lundquist, Per Thorén
1925, Swedish language book

Trondhjems skøiteklub: 1876 - 24. februar - 1926; en
oversigt over foreningens virksomhet
N. Wefring
1926, Norwegian language book

The Glencoe Club 1931-1981
The Glencoe Club
1931

60 Jahre Sportplatz: Engelmann im auftrage des Vereines
Kunsteisbahn Engelmann
Alexander Meisel
1932, German language book

Cambridge Skating Club, 1898-1948
Arthur M. Goodridge
1948

Oslo skøyteklubb gjennom 50 år: 1898-1948
Finn Amundsen, Oslo skøyteklubb
1948, Norwegian language book

One Hundred Years of the Philadelphia Skating Club
and Humane Society

William Morris Maier
1949

The Book of the Old Edinburgh Club, Volume XXXIII, Part 2
Margaret Elliot
1971, chapter on the Edinburgh Skating Club's history (1778-1966)

På skøyter i 100 år: en historisk oversikt
Tore Jacobsen, Trondhjem Skøiteklub
1976, Norwegian language book

The Pleasure of The Game: The Story of the Toronto Cricket, Skating and Curling Club
Stanley Fillmore
1977

Oulun Luistinseura 1880-1980
Kullervo Leinonen, Antti Pesola, Oulun luistinseura
1980, Finnish language book

Hundra år med SASK: Stockholms allmänna skridskoklubb 1883-1983
Elsa Lundberg, Stockholms allmänna skridskoklubb
1983, Swedish language book

The Home Club – The Cleveland Skating Club Story
W.D. Ellis, P.G. Fanslow, N.A. Schneider
1986

KULS, Kuopion luisteluseura 90: 1900-1990

Eevi-Kirsti Järvelä, Kuopion luisteluseura
1990, Finnish language book

Íþróttir í Reykjavík
Sigurð Á Friðþjófsson
1994, Icelandic language book

Helsingin luistelijat r.y. 1908-1993
Riitta Linna, Helsingin luistelijat
1997, Finnish language book

Helsingin työväen luistelijat: seitsemän vuosikymmentä, 1928-1998
Helsingin työväen luistelijat
1998, Finnish language book

早稲田大学スケート部75周年誌: クロちゃんのあゆみ
Waseda University Skating Club
1998, Japanese language book

Carved in Granite: 125 Years of Granite Club History
Rod Austin, Theodore Barris
1999

The Glencoe Club Story: 70 Years of Sports History 1931-2001
Wendy Bryden
2001

A History of the Cambridge Skating Club 1897-2001
Annette LaMond, Cambridge Skating Club
2002

See You On The Ice: A History of the Liverpool Ice Rink
Derek Whale
2002

銀盤の歩み：青森県スケート連盟創立75周年記念誌
Aomori Prefecture Skating Federation
2002, Japanese language book

Vaasan luistinkerho - Vasa skrinnskoklubb ry 1953-2003
Anja Uusikylä, Erkki Salminen, Solveig Håkans, Vaasan luistinkerho
2003, Finnish language book

Kallion luistinrata ry 70 vuotta 1932-2002
Kallion luistinratayhdistys
2003, Finnish language book

Minto: Skating Through Time, 1904-2004
Janet B. Uren
2004

ETK 25 vuotta 1979-2004: Espoon taitoluistelukulubi ry:n juhlakirja
Hanni Kantele, Riitta-Leena Roos, Kirsi Virkkunen, Espoon taitoluistelukulubi
2004, Finnish language book

長野県スケート連盟史：創立60周年記念誌
Nagano Prefecture Skating Federation
2005, Japanese language book

東北大学スケート部八十年史
Tohoku University Skating Club
2010, Japanese language book

History of Southampton Ice Dance & Figure Skating Club, 1952-1988
Eileen de Lisle Long, Brian Cox
2011

Lake Placid Figure Skating: A History
Christie Sausa
2012

The Most Famous Ice Rink in the World: Memories of Richmond Ice Rink
Jeremy Hamilton-Miller
2015

東京大学スケート部アイスホッケー部門 90 年史
University of Tokyo Skating Club
2015, Japanese language book

Karlskrona Allmänna Skridskoklubb 50 år, 1964-2014: en liten historiebok
Lotta Kihlbert, Karlskrona Allmänna Skridskoklubb
2015, Swedish language book

150 Jahre Eiszeit: Die Grosse Geschichte Des Wiener Eislauf-Vereins
Agnes Meisinger
2017

SKATING IN ART

For centuries, artists have drawn inspiration from skating and vice versa. From paintings to sculptures to architecture, these books offer a fascinating perspective on skating art.

Der Eislauf in kunsthistorischer Darstellung
George Helfrich
1903, German language book

Toller
Elva Oglanby
1976

Skating in the Arts of 17th Century Holland: An Exhibition Honoring the 1987 World Figure Skating Championships
Laurinda S. Dixon, The Taft Museum
1987

A Dictionary of Sporting Artists: 1650-1990
Mary Ann Wingfield
1992

The Skating Minister: The Man Behind The Painting
Duncan Thompson, Lynne Gladstone-Millar
2004

Hendrick Avercamp: Master of the Ice Scene
Pieter Roelofs, Jonathan Bikker, Adriaan de Kraker,

Rijksmuseum, National Gallery of Art
2009

Figure Skating And The Arts: Eight Centuries Of Sport And Inspiration
Frances Dafoe
2011

THE SCIENCE OF SKATING

Want be blinded by science like in that song from the eighties? These fascinating books will do just that!

Anatomisk-fysiologiske undersøkelser av skøiteløpere
P. Torgersen
1915, Danish language book

The Figure Skate: A Research into Dimensions and Their Effects Upon Performance With a Consideration of Penetrations into Ice and the Pressure Upon It
C.S. D'Este Stock
1954

The Basic Principles Of Ice Skating: Biomechanics of Skating, Judgement of a Test or a Competition of Skating
Nghiem Minh Dung
1984

Technik der Eiskunstsprünge: auf biomechanischer, mathematischer und physikalischer Grundlage
Ludvik Marek

1994, German language book

The Science of Figure Skating: An Anthology of 28 Graphs for Kids, Teens & Curious Adults
M. Schottenbauer
2014, children's/young adult book

The Science of Figure Skating
Jason Vescovi, Jaci VanHeest
2018

STEM in Figure Skating
Marne Ventura
2018, children's/young adult book

Breaking the Ice: Breaking Down the Science of Figure Skating Jumps for Effective Training and Injury Prevention
Sophie Paradi
2019

SKATING IN THE MEDIA

Figure skating would simply not enjoy the popularity it does today without the incredible work of journalists and those working in the film and television industries. These books offer a behind-the-scenes glimpse of skating media magic.

ABC's Wide World of Sports: A Panorama of Championship Sport

Irving A. Leitner
1975

Ice Time: A Portrait of Figure Skating
Debbi Wilkes, Greg Cable
1994

CTV: The Network That Means Business
Michael Nolan
2001

Skating on Air: The Broadcast History of an Olympic Marquee Sport
Kelli Lawrence
2011

The World Was Our Stage: Spanning the Globe with ABC Sports
Doug Wilson, Jody Cohan-French
2013

Interesting, Very Interesting
Barry Davies
2014

LGBTQ+ SKATING

LGBTQ+ figure skating history is something to be celebrated from the rooftops. When you're finished reading some of the excellent books about LGBTQ+ skaters in the biography section, give these loud and proud books a read!

A favour while you're at it. If you hear someone say "I don't care about their sexuality... what's important is the skating" please roll your eyes on behalf of every wonderful LGBTQ+ skater out there who deserves every ounce of our support and recognition. Inclusivity is so important and comments like that are incredibly dated and unhelpful.

The Arena of Masculinity: Sports, Homosexuality and The Meaning of Sex
Brian Pronger
1990

Unity: A Celebration of Gay Games IV and Stonewall
Lisa Labrecque
1994

The Lavender Locker Room: 3000 Years of Great Athletes Whose Sexual Orientation Was Different
Patricia Nell Warren
2006

The Gay Games: A History
Caroline Symons
2010

Red Nails, Black Skates: Gender, Cash and Pleasure On and Off The Ice
Erica Rand
2012

Queerly Canadian: An Introductory Reader in Sexuality Studies
Scott Rayter, Laine Halpern Zisman
2012

Sexual Minorities in Sports: Prejudice at Play
Melanie L. Sartore-Baldwin
2013

Pirouetten
Tillie Walden
2018, German language book

ACADEMIA

Scholarly perspectives on skating are a very rare treat. The intersection of tried, tested and true research methods and good writing have resulted in some excellent books on skating over the years.

I would also highly recommend checking out resources like ProQuest Dissertations and Theses, Center for Research Libraries and Google Scholar. You will be shocked at how many excellent dissertations and theses on skating have been penned over the years, the majority on extremely specific skating-related topics you won't find covered anywhere else.

I highly suggest reading anything written by German skating historian Dr. Matthias Hampe, as well as Mary

Louise Wright's excellent book "Artistic Impressions: Figure Skating, Masculinity, And The Limits of Sport".

Stilwandel im Eiskunstlauf: eine Ästhetik- und Kulturgeschichte
Dr. Matthias Hampe
1994, German language book

Idrett, medier og kjønnsforskjeller: en undersøkelse av språklige uttrykksmiddel og innholdsmomenter i den omtale mannlige og kvinnelige idrettsutøvere får i dagspressen
Monika Guttormsen
1995, Norwegian language book

Æstetiske idrætsgrene og spiseforstyrrelser - årsager til den store forekomst af spiseforstyrrelser indenfor æstetiske idrætsgrene dyrket på eliteplan
Charlotte R. Petersen
1996, Danish language book, focus on eating disorders in aesthetic sports

Ausdauerfähigkeiten im Eiskunstlaufen, Eistanzen
Dr. Matthias Hampe
1996, German language book

Mediated Women: Representations in Popular Culture
Marian Meyers
1999

Reading Sport: Critical Essays on Power and Representation

Susan Birrell, Mary G. McDonald
2000

Sport as Symbol: Images of The Athlete in Art,
Literature and Song
Mari Womack
2003

Culture On Ice: Figure Skating And Cultural Meaning
Ellyn Kestnbaum
2003

Trainings-und Wettkampfforschung im Eiskunstlaufen:
komplexe prozessbegleitende Trainings- und
Wettkampfforschung in den technisch-kompositorischen
Sportarten unter besonderer Berücksichtigung des
Eiskunstlaufens
Karen Knoll
2004, German language book

Artistic Impressions: Figure Skating, Masculinity, And
The Limits of Sport
Mary Louise Adams
2011

Sequins and Scandals: Reflections on Figure Skating,
Culture and the Philosophy of Sport
M.G. Piety
2014

Reclaiming Canadian Bodies: Visual Media and
Representation

Lynda Mannik, Karen McGarry
2015

Efekti transformacionih procesa različito struktuiranih programa na uspješnost učenja i usavršavanja stilizovanih kretnih struktura klizanja na ledu
Marijana Podrug Arapović
2016, Serbian language book

COOKING

Though there are only four books listed on this page, skaters have been writing about food for decades!

Maribel Vinson Owen wrote for "American Cookery" magazine back in the 1930's and much more recently, Meagan Duhamel's Lutz of Greens blog has shared some wonderfully nourishing vegan recipes which everyone can enjoy.

Skating clubs around the world have been producing DIY cookbooks for decades as fundraisers. The first mention of a cookbook in "Skating" magazine was the Old York Road Figure Skating Club of Elkin Park, Pennsylvania's "Ice 'n Easy Recipes" in 1971. It featured "a wide variety of recipes, skating-oriented verses and pictures, and exercises to keep that old skating figure."

The next time you're at a book fair, take a look in the cookbook section - you just might find one produced by your local skating club!

A Skating Mom's Cookbook
Kathy Barron
1993

Figure Skaters' Favorites Vol. 1
Michelle Bingham Capron, Glens Falls Figure Skating Club
2009

What Would Brian Boitano Make?: Fresh And Fun Recipes For Sharing With Family And Friends
Brian Boitano
2013

Figure Skaters' Favourites Vol. 2
Michelle Bingham Capron
2020

FASHION

Take a deep dive in the archives of 19th Century newspapers and ladies journals and you will soon realize that skating fashion has been a popular topic for a very long time.

If studying historical skating fashion is something of interest to you, I would recommend not only consulting the books on this list, but taking a look at back issues of the periodicals listed in this book. "American Skating World", in particular, covered this topic extensively.

Vintage photographs, sewing patterns and mail-order catalogues are also wonderful primary sources in this regard.

Lois and Richard Stephenson's "A History and Annotated Bibliography of Skating Costume" is one of the best books on skating fashion, but also one of the hardest to come by. The Toronto Public Library has a copy in their Special Collections.

How To Become A Skater
Frederick R. Toombs
1904

The Handbook Of Skating For Use On The Ice
George Henry Browne
1907

The Book of Winter Sports
Madge and Edgar Syers
1908

The Art of Skating
Irving Brokaw
1913

Hippodrome Skating Book: Practical Illustrations in the Art of Figure Skating
Charlotte Oelschlägel
1916

Figure Skating For Women

James A. Cruikshank
1921

Figure Skating Simplified For Beginners
Major G. Baillie
1922

Maribel Y. Vinson's Primer of Figure Skating
Maribel Vinson Owen
1938

Ice-Skating: A History
Nigel Brown
1959

Touristinder og andre sportspiker; blad av
sportsdraktens og kvinne-emansipasjonens historie
Astrid Scholdager Bugge
1961, Norwegian language book

Sixty Years Of Fashion: 1900-1960, The Evolution of
Women's Styles in America
Alice Lessing, Rhea Bower, Ermina Stimson
1963

Winter Sports
Howard Bass
1968

English Costume For Sports And Outdoor Recreation
From The 16th To The 19th Centuries
Phillis Cunnington, Alan Mansfield

1969

A History and Annotated Bibliography of Skating Costume
Lois and Richard Stephenson
1970

The Encyclopedia of World Costume
Doreen Yarwood
1978

A Survey Of Historic Costume
Phyllis Tortora, Keith Eubank
1989

A Passion To Skate: An Intimate View of Figure Skating
Sandra Bezic, David Hayes
1996

The Official Book of Figure Skating
Mary Tiegreen, ABC Sports, U.S. Figure Skating Association
1998

Figure Skating and The Arts: Eight Centuries of Sport and Inspiration
Frances Dafoe
2011

Spandex, Simplified: Sewing For Skaters
Marie Porter
2012

Figure Skating Art Costumes
Satomi Ito
2020, Japanese language book

FICTION, CHILDREN'S BOOKS, ETC.

Skating fiction has been around a very long time and there are some notable examples of outstanding writing in this field. Mary Mapes Dodge's "Hans Brinker, or The Silver Skates", first published in 1865, has been translated into numerous languages and enjoyed by readers around the world for over a century. Dick Button even skated in its first adaptation for North American television in 1958. Tenley Albright's daughter Elee penned a gorgeous book of skating poetry called "Serpentine Loop" which I would highly recommend. Even Margaret Atwood herself penned a skating-themed poem for her 1970 poetry book "Procedures for Underground".

If skating fiction is your thing, there are mysteries, romances and dramas galore aplenty out there and major online book retailers are a great place to start looking. Quite frankly, they are not catalogued in this bibliography as the book is big enough as it is.
This bibliography is primarily meant to be a resource for historical research. The biography section of this book includes books geared towards children and young adults, but I have chosen to exclude many general skating books for younger readers from the general section. Though charming at times, they really don't

offer information that can't be found elsewhere.

There are hundreds of general books about the Olympic Games which contain important historical information about the sport. The LA84 Foundation's Digital Library is a phenomenal place to start your quest for Olympic books.

BIOGRAPHIES

Unlike the other books in this section, which are categorized by year, the listing of biographies is listed by skater.

I would highly recommend you also check out Skate Guard blog at <http://skateguard1.blogspot.ca> as well, as biographical material of dozens of these skaters can be found there as well. A prime example is the feature "All The Best, Belita" on Belita Jepson-Turner, which is far more extensive than any of the print entries in this listing.

Adam Rippon

Beautiful On The Outside: A Memoir
Adam Rippon, 2019

Adelina Sotnikova

Сердце льда: для влюбленных в фигурное катание
Adelina Sotnikova, 2020, Russian language book

Ája Vrzáňová

Kariéra: vzpomínky Ája Vrzáňová
Ája Vrzáňová, Svatava Chalupská, 2000, Czech language book

Na bruslích do světa
Ája Vrzáňová, Alena Kohoutova, 1993, Czech language book

Ice Skating
T.D. Richardson, 1956

Akiko Suzuki

等身大」で生きる—スケートで学んだチャンスのつかみ方
Akiko Suzuki, 2015, Japanese language book

笑顔が未来をつくる—私のスケート人生
Akiko Suzuki, 2015, Japanese language book

壁はきっと越えられる—夢をかなえる晩成力
Akiko Suzuki, 2014, Japanese language book

アイスモデリスト
Junko Yaginuma, 2012, Japanese language book

ひとつひとつ。少しずつ
Akiko Suzuki, 2014, Japanese language book

Alain Calmat

Vivre mieux par la sport
Alain Calmat, 1981, French language book, though about health and sport, this book contains autobiographical elements

Les Riches Heures du Patinage
Jean-Christophe Berlot, 2002, French language book

Alan Weeks

Another Slice of Johnners
Brian Johnston, 2012

Albena Denkova and Maxim Staviski

Figure Skating Today: The Next Wave of Stars
Steve Milton, Gérard Châtaigneau, 2007

Любов е алхимията на успеха
Albena Denkova, 2006, Bulgarian language book

Alexandra Trusova

Александра Трусова. Девочка, победившая гравитацию
Elena Zotova, 2020, Russian language book

Alexei Mishin

Слезы на льду
Elena Vaitsekhovskaya, 2007, Russian language book

Алексей Мишин 6.0
L. Chernyshova, 2017, Russian language book

О чем молчит лед? О жизни и карьере великого тренера
Alexei Mishin, 2019, Russian language book

Alexei Urmanov

Super Skaters: World Figure Skating Stars
Steve Milton, 1994, children's/young adult book

Ice Stars: A Celebration of the Artistry, Beauty and Grace of the Ice-Skating World
Kevin Bursey, 1999

Alexei Yagudin

Figure Skating's Greatest Stars
Steve Milton, 2009

Figure Skating Champions
Steve Milton, Gérard Châtaigneau, 2002, children's/young adult book

Слезы на льду
Elena Vaitsekhovskaya, 2007, Russian language book

Фигурное катание. Только звезды
Elena Vaitsekhovskaya, Alexander Wilf, 2008, Russian language book

"НаPRолом" Прауз Линда, Ягудин Алексей
Alexei Yagudin, Lynda Prouse, 2008, Russian language book

Ice Stars: A Celebration of the Artistry, Beauty and Grace of the Ice-Skating World
Kevin Bursey, 1999

Alina Zagitova

Фигурное катание. Стальные девочки
Elena Vaitsekhovskaya, 2020, Russian language book

Aliona Savchenko, Robin Szolkowy and Bruno Massot

Der lange Weg zum olympischen Gold
Alexandra Illina, 2020, German language book

Figure Skating Today: The Next Wave of Stars
Steve Milton, Gérard Châtaigneau, 2007

Chemnitz Eissterne
Martina Martin, 2010, German language book

Ein perfektes Paar
Tatjana Flade, 2016, German language book

Alissa Czisny

Figure Skating Today: The Next Wave of Stars
Steve Milton, Gérard Châtaigneau, 2007

Alois Lutz

Lutz
Jim Palette, 2021, French language book, historical fiction biopic

Andrea Gardiner

Black Firsts: 4,000 Ground-breaking and Pioneering Historical Events
Jessie Carney Smith, 2003

Andrée and Pierre Brunet

Figure Skating's Greatest Stars
Steve Milton, 2009

The Official Book of Figure Skating
U.S. Figure Skating Association, 1998

Ice Skating
T.D. Richardson, 1956

Reader's Guide To Figure Skating's Hall of Fame
Benjamin T. Wright, Gregory Smith, U.S. Figure Skating Association, 1978

Les Riches Heures du Patinage
Jean-Christophe Berlot, 2002, French language book

Anett Pötzsch

Chemnitz Eissterne
Martina Martin, 2010, German language book

Angelika Krylova and Oleg Ovsiannikov

Skate Talk: Figure Skating In The Words Of The Stars
Steve Milton, 1998

Ice Stars: A Celebration of the Artistry, Beauty and Grace of the Ice-Skating World
Kevin Bursey, 1999

Annie Barabé

Taking The Ice: Success Stories from the World of Canadian Figure Skating
PJ Kwong, 2010

Arthur Cumming

Yesterday's Child, 1890-1909
Beryl Lee Booker, 1937

Our Skating Heritage
Dennis L. Bird, 1979

Atoy Wilson

Black Firsts: 4,000 Ground-breaking and Pioneering Historical Events
Jessie Carney Smith, 2003

Audrey Weisiger

Skating With The World
Joanne Vassallo Jamrosz, 2014

Still Skating Forward: Amazing People Celebrating Life and Skating
Joanne Vassallo Jamrosz, 2012

Axel Paulsen

Op glad ijs : over schaatsen en schaatsenrijders
H.J. Looman, 1948, Dutch language book

Isens helter med skøyteløperne verden rundt
Peder Christian Andersen, 1941, Norwegian language book

Figure Skating's Greatest Stars
Steve Milton, 2009

Reader's Guide To Figure Skating's Hall of Fame
Benjamin T. Wright, Gregory Smith, U.S. Figure Skating Association, 1978

The Skating Scene: Champions & Championships, The Fact Book of Skating
Arthur R. Goodfellow, 1981

Barbara Ann Scott

Figure Skating: A Celebration
Beverley Smith, 1994

Figure Skating's Greatest Stars
Steve Milton, 2009

The Golden Age of Canadian Figure Skating
David Young, 1984

Skate Talk: Figure Skating In The Words Of The Stars
Steve Milton, 1998

Skate With Me
Barbara Ann Scott, 1950

She Skated Into Our Hearts
Cay Moore, Donald B. Cruikshank, Osborne Colson, 1948

Ice Stars: A Celebration of the Artistry, Beauty and Grace of the Ice-Skating World
Kevin Bursey, 1999

Ice Skating
T.D. Richardson, 1956

Legendary Canadian Women
Carol McLeod, 1983

Minto: Skating Through Time, History of the Minto Skating Club 1904-2004
Janet B. Uren, 2004

Sport in Canada: A History
Don Morrow, Kevin B. Wamsley, 2005

The Girl and The Game: A History of Women's Sport in Canada
Margaret Anne Hall, 2002

Whatever Became Of?
Richard Lamparski, 1967

Taking The Ice: Success Stories from the World of Canadian Figure Skating
PJ Kwong, 2010

Barbara Underhill and Paul Martini

Figure Skating's Greatest Stars
Steve Milton, 2009

The Golden Age of Canadian Figure Skating
David Young, 1984

Skate Talk: Figure Skating In The Words Of The Stars
Steve Milton, 1998

Skate: 100 Years Of Figure Skating
Steve Milton, Barbara McCutcheon, 1996

Ice Stars: A Celebration of the Artistry, Beauty and Grace of the Ice-Skating World
Kevin Bursey, 1999

The Passion To Skate: An Intimate View Of Figure Skating
Sandra Bezic, 1996

Entering the mother zone: Balancing self, health & family
Alexandra Powe Allred, 2000

Chicken Soup for the Soul: Living your Dreams, Inspirational Stories, Powerful Principles, and Practical Techniques to Help Make Your Dreams Come True
Jack Canfield, Mark Victor Hansen, 2003

Taking The Ice: Success Stories from the World of Canadian Figure Skating
PJ Kwong, 2010

Barbara Wagner and Robert Paul

Figure Skating's Greatest Stars
Steve Milton, 2009

The Golden Age of Canadian Figure Skating
David Young, 1984

Beatrix Loughran and Sherwin Badger

Reader's Guide To Figure Skating's Hall of Fame
Benjamin T. Wright, Gregory Smith, U.S. Figure Skating Association, 1978

Belita Jepson-Turner

No Wonder I Like Butterflies: A Life of Travel
Patricia Margaret, 2013

What Became Of...? (Fourth Series)
Richard Lamparski, 1973

Earl's Court
Claude Langdon, 1953

Beverley Smith

Skate Talk: Figure Skating In The Words Of The Stars
Steve Milton, 1998

Bill Kipp

Indelible Tracings: The Story of the 1961 U.S. World
Figure Skating Team
Patricia Shelley Bushman, 2010

Indelible Images: An Illustrated History Of The 1961
U.S. World Figure Skating Team
Patricia Shelley Bushman, 2011

Frozen in Time: The Enduring Legacy of the 1961 U.S.
Figure Skating Team
Nikki Nichols, 2008

Bill Swallender

Indelible Tracings: The Story of the 1961 U.S. World
Figure Skating Team
Patricia Shelley Bushman, 2010

Indelible Images: An Illustrated History Of The 1961
U.S. World Figure Skating Team
Patricia Shelley Bushman, 2011

Frozen in Time: The Enduring Legacy of the 1961 U.S.
Figure Skating Team
Nikki Nichols, 2008

Bradley Lord

Indelible Tracings: The Story of the 1961 U.S. World
Figure Skating Team
Patricia Shelley Bushman, 2010

Indelible Images: An Illustrated History Of The 1961
U.S. World Figure Skating Team
Patricia Shelley Bushman, 2011

Frozen in Time: The Enduring Legacy of the 1961 U.S.
Figure Skating Team
Nikki Nichols, 2008

Brian Boitano

Ice Skating: From Axels to Zambonis
Dan Gutman, 1995, children's/young adult book

Figure Skating's Greatest Stars

Steve Milton, 2009

Super Skaters: World Figure Skating Stars
Steve Milton, 1994, children's/young adult book

Skate Talk: Figure Skating In The Words Of The Stars
Steve Milton, 1998

Skate: 100 Years Of Figure Skating
Steve Milton, Barbara McCutcheon, 1996

Boitano's Edge: Inside The Real World Of Figure Skating
Brian Boitano, Suzanne Harper, 1997

Ice Stars: A Celebration of the Artistry, Beauty and Grace of the Ice-Skating World
Kevin Bursey, 1999

The Official Book of Figure Skating
U.S. Figure Skating Association, 1998

Brian Joubert

Figure Skating Today: The Next Wave of Stars
Steve Milton, Gérard Châtaigneau, 2007

Brian Joubert sur papier glacé
Brian Joubert, Loïc Lejay, 2010, French language book

Brian Orser

Ice Cream: Thirty of the Most Interesting Skaters in History
Toller Cranston, Martha Lowder Kimball, 2002

Figure Skating's Greatest Stars
Steve Milton, 2009

Skate Talk: Figure Skating In The Words Of The Stars
Steve Milton, 1998

Brian Orser
Stephanie Papp Geddes, Brian Geddes, 1998, children's/young adult book

Orser: A Skater's Life
Brian Orser, Steve Milton, 1988

Taking The Ice: Success Stories from the World of Canadian Figure Skating
PJ Kwong, 2010

Bror Meyer

Ice Skating
T.D. Richardson, 1956

Carlo Fassi

Talking Figure Skating: Behind The Scenes in the World's Most Glamourous Sport
Beverley Smith, 1997

The Official Book of Figure Skating
U.S. Figure Skating Association, 1998

Carol Heiss Jenkins

Ice Skating: From Axels to Zambonis
Dan Gutman, 1995, children's/young adult book

Figure Skating's Greatest Stars
Steve Milton, 2009

Golden Skates: The Story Of Carol Heiss, Teen-Age Champion
Helen Cambria Bolstad, 1960

Carol Heiss, Olympic Queen
Robert Parker, 1961

The Official Book of Figure Skating
U.S. Figure Skating Association, 1998

Reader's Guide To Figure Skating's Hall of Fame
Benjamin T. Wright, Gregory Smith, U.S. Figure Skating Association, 1978

Skate Talk: Figure Skating In The Words Of The Stars
Steve Milton, 1998

Carolina Kostner

Figure Skating Today: The Next Wave of Stars
Steve Milton, Gérard Châtaigneau, 2007

Caryn Kadavy

Skating With The World
Joanne Vassallo Jamrosz, 2014

Cathy Dalton

Taking The Ice: Success Stories from the World of Canadian Figure Skating
PJ Kwong, 2010

Cecil Smith

The Golden Age of Canadian Figure Skating
David Young, 1984

The Girl and The Game: A History of Women's Sport in Canada
Margaret Anne Hall, 2002

Cecilia Colledge
Earl's Court
Claude Langdon, 1953

Die Eisparade: Meisterinnen auf Schlittschuhen, wie sie sind und wie sie wurden, Kampf um den Weltmeisterthron
Hans Saalbach, 1938, German language book

Ice Skating
T.D. Richardson, 1956

Skaters' Cavalcade: Fifty Years of Skating
A.C.A. Wade, 1939

Britain's Olympic Women: A History
Jean Williams, 2021

Our Skating Heritage
Dennis L. Bird, 1979

Chantal Loyer and Justin Bell

Olympic Dream: The Pain and Glory of Figure Skating
Penelope Barbe, 2009

Charles Cumming

Minto: Skating Through Time, History of the Minto Skating Club 1904-2004
Janet B. Uren, 2004

Charlie Tickner

Winners On The Ice (A Picture Life Book)
Frank Litsky, 1979, children's/young adult book

The Official Book of Figure Skating
U.S. Figure Skating Association, 1998

Charlotte Oelschlägel

Ice Skating: From Axels to Zambonis

Dan Gutman, 1995, children's/young adult book

Figure Skating: A Celebration
Beverley Smith, 1994

Figure Skating For Women
James A. Cruikshank, 1921

Admiralspalast: Die Geschichte eines Berliner
Jost Lehne, 2006

Ice-Skating: A History
Nigel Brown, 1959

The Skating Scene: Champions & Championships, The Fact Book of Skating
Arthur R. Goodfellow, 1981

Christopher Bowman

Ice Skating: From Axels to Zambonis
Dan Gutman, 1995, children's/young adult book

Talking Figure Skating: Behind The Scenes in the World's Most Glamourous Sport
Beverley Smith, 1997

Daisuke Takahashi

Figure Skating Today: The Next Wave of Stars
Steve Milton, Gérard Châtaigneau, 2007

髙橋大輔写真集 The Long and Winding Road
Shinkoshan, 2020, Japanese language photo book

髙橋大輔写真集　艶技2019
Pony Canyon, 2019, Japanese language photo book

髙橋大輔写真集 氷艶2017『艶技』
Pony Canyon, 2019, Japanese language photo book

2000 days—-過ごした日々が僕を進ませる
Shodensha, 2015, Japanese language book

それでも前を向くために be SOUL 2
Shodensha, 2013, Japanese language book

SOUL Up Exhibition
祥伝社
Shodensha, 2011, Japanese language book

SOUL Up 祥伝社
Shodensha, 2011, Japanese language book

STEP！STEP！STEP！ 髙橋大輔―フィギュアスケートを行
Nihon Keizai Shimbun, 2011, Japanese language book

髙橋大輔OFFICIAL BOOK 200days バンクーバーまでの闘い（祥伝社
Shodensha, 2010, Japanese language book

be SOUL（祥伝社
Shodensha, 2010, Japanese language book

アイスモデリスト
Junko Yaginuma, 2012, Japanese language book

ボクらの時代 自分を「美しく」見せる技術（藤原竜也
Daisuke Takahashi, Tatsuya Fujiwara, Kantaro Nakamura, 2008, Japanese language book

Danny Ryan

Indelible Tracings: The Story of the 1961 U.S. World Figure Skating Team
Patricia Shelley Bushman, 2010

Indelible Images: An Illustrated History Of The 1961 U.S. World Figure Skating Team
Patricia Shelley Bushman, 2011

Frozen in Time: The Enduring Legacy of the 1961 U.S. Figure Skating Team
Nikki Nichols, 2008

Daphne Walker

Skaters' Cavalcade: Fifty Years of Skating
A.C.A. Wade, 1939

Our Skating Heritage
Dennis L. Bird, 1979

David Dore

Skate Talk: Figure Skating In The Words Of The Stars

Steve Milton, 1998

David Jenkins

Figure Skating's Greatest Stars
Steve Milton, 2009

The Official Book of Figure Skating
U.S. Figure Skating Association, 1998

Reader's Guide To Figure Skating's Hall of Fame
Benjamin T. Wright, Gregory Smith, U.S. Figure Skating Association, 1978

The Skating Scene: Champions & Championships, The Fact Book of Skating
Arthur R. Goodfellow, 1981

David Santee

Skating With The World
Joanne Vassallo Jamrosz, 2014

David Wilson

Taking The Ice: Success Stories from the World of Canadian Figure Skating
PJ Kwong, 2010

Deane McMinn

Indelible Tracings: The Story of the 1961 U.S. World

Figure Skating Team
Patricia Shelley Bushman, 2010

Indelible Images: An Illustrated History Of The 1961 U.S. World Figure Skating Team
Patricia Shelley Bushman, 2011

Frozen in Time: The Enduring Legacy of the 1961 U.S. Figure Skating Team
Nikki Nichols, 2008

Debbi Wilkes and Guy Revell

Skate Talk: Figure Skating In The Words Of The Stars
Steve Milton, 1998

Ice Time: A Portrait of Figure Skating
Debbi Wilkes, Greg Cable, 1994

Taking The Ice: Success Stories from the World of Canadian Figure Skating
PJ Kwong, 2010

Debi Thomas

Debi Thomas: What Really Happened
Carol Denise Mitchell, 2020

The Official Book of Figure Skating
U.S. Figure Skating Association, 1998

Rivals: Legendary Matchups That Made Sports History

David Kenneth Wiggins, Pierre R. Rodgers, 2010

Black Firsts: 4,000 Ground-breaking and Pioneering Historical Events
Jessie Carney Smith, 2003

Denis Ten

Nash Denis
Ministry of Culture and Sport of the Republic of Kazakhstan, 2018, Kazakh language book

Denise Biellmann

Denise Biellmann: Die Biografie
Denise Biellmann, 2022, German language book

Diane Sherbloom and Dallas 'Larry' Pierce

Indelible Tracings: The Story of the 1961 U.S. World Figure Skating Team
Patricia Shelley Bushman, 2010

Indelible Images: An Illustrated History Of The 1961 U.S. World Figure Skating Team
Patricia Shelley Bushman, 2011

Frozen in Time: The Enduring Legacy of the 1961 U.S. Figure Skating Team
Nikki Nichols, 2008

Diane Towler and Bernard Ford

Figure Skating: A Celebration
Beverley Smith, 1994

Figure Skating's Greatest Stars
Steve Milton, 2009

Ice Stars: A Celebration of the Artistry, Beauty and Grace of the Ice-Skating World
Kevin Bursey, 1999

Dianne de Leeuw

Figure Skating
Elizabeth van Steenwyk, 1976, children's/young adult book

Dick Button

Ice Skating: From Axels to Zambonis
Dan Gutman, 1995, children's/young adult book

Figure Skating's Greatest Stars
Steve Milton, 2009

Skate: 100 Years Of Figure Skating
Steve Milton, Barbara McCutcheon, 1996

Edge Is a Lean of the Body: A Memoir of Skating
Dick Button, 2001

Winners On The Ice (A Picture Life Book)

Frank Litsky, 1979, children's/young adult book

Push Dick's Button: A Conversation On Skating From A Good Part Of The Last Century - And A Little Tomfoolery
Dick Button, 2013, while mostly a conversation about figure skating in general, does include autobiographical elements

Dick Button On Skates
Dick Button, 1955

Ice Stars: A Celebration of the Artistry, Beauty and Grace of the Ice-Skating World
Kevin Bursey, 1999

The Official Book of Figure Skating
U.S. Figure Skating Association, 1998

Championship Figure Skating: The Famous System of Gustave Lussi
Gustave Lussi, Maurice Richards, 1951

Ice Skating
T.D. Richardson, 1956

Ice-Skating: A History
Nigel Brown, 1959

Reader's Guide To Figure Skating's Hall of Fame
Benjamin T. Wright, Gregory Smith, U.S. Figure Skating Association, 1978

Les Riches Heures du Patinage
Jean-Christophe Berlot, 2002, French language book

Don Laws

Don Laws: The Life Of An Olympic Figure Skating Coach
Beverly Ann Menke, 2012

Dona Lee Carrier, Roger and Ann Campbell

Indelible Tracings: The Story of the 1961 U.S. World Figure Skating Team
Patricia Shelley Bushman, 2010

Indelible Images: An Illustrated History Of The 1961 U.S. World Figure Skating Team
Patricia Shelley Bushman, 2011

Frozen in Time: The Enduring Legacy of the 1961 U.S. Figure Skating Team
Nikki Nichols, 2008

Donald B. Cruikshank

Minto: Skating Through Time, History of the Minto Skating Club 1904-2004
Janet B. Uren, 2004

Donald Jackson

Figure Skating: A Celebration
Beverley Smith, 1994

Figure Skating's Greatest Stars
Steve Milton, 2009

The Golden Age of Canadian Figure Skating
David Young, 1984

Skate: 100 Years Of Figure Skating
Steve Milton, Barbara McCutcheon, 1996

Donald Jackson: King Of Blades
George Gross, 1977

Reader's Guide To Figure Skating's Hall of Fame
Benjamin T. Wright, Gregory Smith, U.S. Figure Skating Association, 1978

Minto: Skating Through Time, History of the Minto Skating Club 1904-2004
Janet B. Uren, 2004

Taking The Ice: Success Stories from the World of Canadian Figure Skating
PJ Kwong, 2010

Donald McPherson

The Golden Age of Canadian Figure Skating
David Young, 1984

Donald Tobin

Minto: Skating Through Time, History of the Minto Skating Club 1904-2004
Janet B. Uren, 2004

Dorothy and Hazel Caley

The Girl and The Game: A History of Women's Sport in Canada
Margaret Anne Hall, 2002

Dorothy Greenhough Smith

Ice Skating
T.D. Richardson, 1956

Dorothy Hamill

Ice Skating: From Axels to Zambonis
Dan Gutman, 1995, children's/young adult book

Ice Cream: Thirty of the Most Interesting Skaters in History
Toller Cranston, Martha Lowder Kimball, 2002

Figure Skating's Greatest Stars
Steve Milton, 2009

Dorothy Hamill: Olympic Skating Champion
Edward F. Dolan, 1979, children's/young adult book

Dorothy Hamill
S.H. Burchard, 1978, children's/young adult book

Dorothy Hamill
Miranda Smith, 1977, children's/young adult book

Winners On The Ice (A Picture Life Book)
Frank Litsky, 1979, children's/young adult book

Sports Immortals: Dorothy Hamill
William R. Sanford, Carl R. Green, 1993, children's/young adult book

Figure Skating
Elizabeth van Steenwyk, 1976, children's/young adult book

Dorothy Hamill: Olympic Champion
Elizabeth van Steenwyk, 1976, children's/young adult book

Dorothy Hamill: On And Off The Ice
Dorothy Hamill, Elva (Oglanby) Clairmont, 1983

A Skating Life: My Story
Dorothy Hamill, Deborah Amelon, 2007

The Official Book of Figure Skating
U.S. Figure Skating Association, 1998

Dorothy Jenkins

Minto: Skating Through Time, History of the Minto Skating Club 1904-2004
Janet B. Uren, 2004

Doug Leigh

Talking Figure Skating: Behind The Scenes in the World's Most Glamourous Sport
Beverley Smith, 1997

Taking The Ice: Success Stories from the World of Canadian Figure Skating
PJ Kwong, 2010

Doug Wilson

The World Was Our Stage: Spanning the Globe with ABC Sports
Doug Wilson, 2013

Douglas Ramsay

Indelible Tracings: The Story of the 1961 U.S. World Figure Skating Team
Patricia Shelley Bushman, 2010

Indelible Images: An Illustrated History Of The 1961 U.S. World Figure Skating Team
Patricia Shelley Bushman, 2011

Frozen in Time: The Enduring Legacy of the 1961 U.S. Figure Skating Team

Nikki Nichols, 2008

Eddie and Richard LeMaire

Indelible Tracings: The Story of the 1961 U.S. World Figure Skating Team
Patricia Shelley Bushman, 2010

Indelible Images: An Illustrated History Of The 1961 U.S. World Figure Skating Team
Patricia Shelley Bushman, 2011

Frozen in Time: The Enduring Legacy of the 1961 U.S. Figure Skating Team
Nikki Nichols, 2008

Eddie Shipstad and Oscar Johnson

Reader's Guide To Figure Skating's Hall of Fame
Benjamin T. Wright, Gregory Smith, U.S. Figure Skating Association, 1978

The Skating Scene: Champions & Championships, The Fact Book of Skating
Arthur R. Goodfellow, 1981

Eddie Shipstad, Ice Follies Star
L.E. Leipold, 1971

Edi Scholdan

Indelible Tracings: The Story of the 1961 U.S. World

Figure Skating Team
Patricia Shelley Bushman, 2010

Indelible Images: An Illustrated History Of The 1961 U.S. World Figure Skating Team
Patricia Shelley Bushman, 2011

Frozen in Time: The Enduring Legacy of the 1961 U.S. Figure Skating Team
Nikki Nichols, 2008

Reader's Guide To Figure Skating's Hall of Fame
Benjamin T. Wright, Gregory Smith, U.S. Figure Skating Association, 1978

Ekaterina Gordeeva and Sergei Grinkov

Skate Talk: Figure Skating In The Words Of The Stars
Steve Milton, 1998

Ekaterina Gordeeva: Solo Flight
Gregory Nicoll, 2000, children's/young adult book

Ekaterina Gordeeva: Overcoming Adversity
Anne E. Hill, 2001, children's/young adult book

A Letter For Daria
Ekaterina Gordeeva, Antonina W. Bouis, 1998, children's/young adult book

My Sergei: A Love Story
Ekaterina Gordeeva, E.M. Swift, 1996

Ice Skating: From Axels to Zambonis
Dan Gutman, 1995, children's/young adult book

They Died Too Young: Sergei Grinkov
Anne E. Hill, 2001, children's/young adult book

Figure Skating: A Celebration
Beverley Smith, 1994

Figure Skating's Greatest Stars
Steve Milton, 2009

Super Skaters: World Figure Skating Stars
Steve Milton, 1994, children's/young adult book

Skate: 100 Years Of Figure Skating
Steve Milton, Barbara McCutcheon, 1996

Слезы на льду
Elena Vaitsekhovskaya, 2007, Russian language book

Ice Stars: A Celebration of the Artistry, Beauty and Grace of the Ice-Skating World
Kevin Bursey, 1999

The Official Book of Figure Skating
U.S. Figure Skating Association, 1998

Elaine Zayak

Figure Skating: A Celebration

Beverley Smith, 1994

The Official Book of Figure Skating
U.S. Figure Skating Association, 1998

Eleanor Kingsford

Minto: Skating Through Time, History of the Minto Skating Club 1904-2004
Janet B. Uren, 2004

Eleanor O'Meara

The Girl and The Game: A History of Women's Sport in Canada
Margaret Anne Hall, 2002

Elena Bechke and Denis Petrov

Skate Talk: Figure Skating In The Words Of The Stars
Steve Milton, 1998

Elena Berezhnaya and Anton Sikharulidze

Figure Skating's Greatest Stars
Steve Milton, 2009

Figure Skating Champions
Steve Milton, Gérard Châtaigneau, 2002, children's/young adult book

Слезы на льду

Elena Vaitsekhovskaya, 2007, Russian language book

The Second Mark: Courage, Corruption, and the Battle for Olympic Gold
Joy Goodwin, 2007, though about the judging scandal at the 2002 Winter Olympic Games, this book has strong biographical elements

Ice Stars: A Celebration of the Artistry, Beauty and Grace of the Ice-Skating World
Kevin Bursey, 1999

Elena Chaikovskaya

Слезы на льду
Elena Vaitsekhovskaya, 2007, Russian language book

Конек Чайковской. Обратная сторона медалей
Elena Chaikovskaya, 2017, Russian language book

Elizabeth Manley

Skating With The World
Joanne Vassallo Jamrosz, 2014

Ice Cream: Thirty of the Most Interesting Skaters in History
Toller Cranston, Martha Lowder Kimball, 2002

Skate Talk: Figure Skating In The Words Of The Stars
Steve Milton, 1998

As I Am: My Life After The Olympics
Elizabeth Manley, Lynda Prouse, 2002

Thumbs Up! The Elizabeth Manley Story
Elizabeth Manley, Elva (Oglanby) Clairmont, 1990

Taking The Ice: Success Stories from the World of Canadian Figure Skating
PJ Kwong, 2010

Elizabeth Punsalan and Jerod Swallow

The Official Book of Figure Skating
U.S. Figure Skating Association, 1998

Ellen Burka

Taking The Ice: Success Stories from the World of Canadian Figure Skating
PJ Kwong, 2010

Elvis Stojko

Ice Skating: From Axels to Zambonis
Dan Gutman, 1995, children's/young adult book

Figure Skating: A Celebration
Beverley Smith, 1994

Figure Skating's Greatest Stars
Steve Milton, 2009

Super Skaters: World Figure Skating Stars
Steve Milton, 1994, children's/young adult book

Skate Talk: Figure Skating In The Words Of The Stars
Steve Milton, 1998

Figure Skating Champions
Steve Milton, Gérard Châtaigneau, 2002,
children's/young adult book

Elvis Stojko: Skating From The Blade
Linda Shaughnessy, 1997, children's/young adult book

Heart And Soul
Elvis Stojko, Gérard Châtaigneau, 1997
Elvis Stojko

Ice Stars: A Celebration of the Artistry, Beauty and
Grace of the Ice-Skating World
Kevin Bursey, 1999

The Official Book of Figure Skating
U.S. Figure Skating Association, 1998

Taking The Ice: Success Stories from the World of
Canadian Figure Skating
PJ Kwong, 2010

Emanuel Sandhu

Figure Skating Today: The Next Wave of Stars
Steve Milton, Gérard Châtaigneau, 2007

Emi Watanabe

渡部絵美のちょう美人宣言
Emi Watanabe, 1985, Japanese language book

Emmerich Danzer

Traumfabrik auf dem Eis: Von der Wiener Eisrevue zu Holiday on Ice
Bernhard Hachleitner, Isabella Lechner, 2014, German language book

Emmy Puzinger and Fernand Leemans

Traumfabrik auf dem Eis: Von der Wiener Eisrevue zu Holiday on Ice
Bernhard Hachleitner, Isabella Lechner, 2014, German language book

Eteri Tutberidze

Нельзя останавливаться. Этери Тутберидзе
Alexander Golovin, 2020, Russian language book

Etsuko Inada

稲田悦子伝 ヒトラーと握手した唯一の日本の少女
Yoko Umeda, 2021, Japanese language book

Die Eisparade: Meisterinnen auf Schlittschuhen, wie sie sind und wie sie wurden, Kampf um den

Weltmeisterthron
Hans Saalbach, 1938, German language book

Eva Pawlik and Rudi Seeliger

Traumfabrik auf dem Eis: Von der Wiener Eisrevue zu Holiday on Ice
Bernhard Hachleitner, Isabella Lechner, 2014, German language book

Der Wiener Eisrevue: Einst Botschafterin Österreichs - heute Legende
Dr. Roman Seeliger, 2008, German language book, German language book

Eva Romanová and Pavel Roman

Figure Skating's Greatest Stars
Steve Milton, 2009

Memoir of Eva Romanová
Gillian Oliverová, Alice Lily Neradová, 2021, Czech language book

Eva a Pavel Romanovi
Zdeněk Roman, 1967, Czech language book

Evan Lysacek

Figure Skating Today: The Next Wave of Stars
Steve Milton, Gérard Châtaigneau, 2007

Evelyn Chandler

The Skating Scene: Champions & Championships, The Fact Book of Skating
Arthur R. Goodfellow, 1981

Evgeni Plushenko

Figure Skating's Greatest Stars
Steve Milton, 2009

Figure Skating Champions
Steve Milton, Gérard Châtaigneau, 2002, children's/young adult book

Слезы на льду
Elena Vaitsekhovskaya, 2007, Russian language book

Фигурное катание. Только звезды
Elena Vaitsekhovskaya, Alexander Wilf, 2008, Russian language book

Евгений Плющенко - Другое шоу
Evgeni Plushenko, 2007, Russian language book

Ice Stars: A Celebration of the Artistry, Beauty and Grace of the Ice-Skating World
Kevin Bursey, 1999

Evgenia Medvedeva

Фигурное катание. Стальные девочки

Elena Vaitsekhovskaya, 2020, Russian language book

Frances Claudet

Minto: Skating Through Time, History of the Minto Skating Club 1904-2004
Janet B. Uren, 2004

Frances Dafoe and Norris Bowden

Figure Skating: A Celebration
Beverley Smith, 1994

Figure Skating's Greatest Stars
Steve Milton, 2009

The Golden Age of Canadian Figure Skating
David Young, 1984

Frank Carroll

Talking Figure Skating: Behind The Scenes in the World's Most Glamourous Sport
Beverley Smith, 1997

Skate Talk: Figure Skating In The Words Of The Stars
Steve Milton, 1998

Freddie Tomlins

Freddie Tomlins: His Life On Skates
Peggy Tomlins, 1947

Skaters' Cavalcade: Fifty Years of Skating
A.C.A. Wade, 1939

Our Skating Heritage
Dennis L. Bird, 1979

Fritzi Burger

Searching For Fritzi
Carol Bergman, 1999

Fumio Igarashi

五十嵐文男の華麗なるフィギュアスケート
Fumio Igarashi, 1998, Japanese language book

Gabriella Papadakis and Guillaume Cizeron

Ma plus belle victoire
Guillaume Cizeron, 2021, French language book

Gabriella Papadakis & Guillaume Cizeron - En or: Les coulisses de nos années olympiques
Gabriella Papadakis, Guillaume Cizeron, Clémentine Blondet, 2022. French language book

Gaby Seyfert

Chemnitz Eissterne
Martina Martin, 2010, German language book

Gary Beacom

Ice Cream: Thirty of the Most Interesting Skaters in History
Toller Cranston, Martha Lowder Kimball, 2002

Talking Figure Skating: Behind The Scenes in the World's Most Glamourous Sport
Beverley Smith, 1997

Gary Beacom's Vade Mecum
Gary Beacom, 2006

Apology
Gary Beacom, 2003

Les Riches Heures du Patinage
Jean-Christophe Berlot, 2002, French language book

Gary Visconti

Falling For The Win
Gary Visconti, 2014

Gerhardt Bubnik

Law and Sport: My Passions: The Life Odyssey of Harvard's first Czech Law Graduate
Gerhardt Bubnik, 2020

Gilbert Fuchs

Ice Skating
T.D. Richardson, 1956

Gillis Grafström

Figure Skating's Greatest Stars
Steve Milton, 2009

Ice Skating
T.D. Richardson, 1956

Modern Figure Skating
T.D. Richardson, 1930

Reader's Guide To Figure Skating's Hall of Fame
Benjamin T. Wright, Gregory Smith, U.S. Figure Skating Association, 1978

Les Riches Heures du Patinage
Jean-Christophe Berlot, 2002, French language book

Gladys Hogg

Figure Skating: A Celebration
Beverley Smith, 1994

Our Skating Heritage
Dennis L. Bird, 1979

Gordon Crossland

A Nobody's Dream Came True

Gordon Crossland, 2018

Gordon Forbes

Minto: Skating Through Time, History of the Minto Skating Club 1904-2004
Janet B. Uren, 2004

Graham Sharp

Skaters' Cavalcade: Fifty Years of Skating
A.C.A. Wade, 1939

Gregory Kelley

Indelible Tracings: The Story of the 1961 U.S. World Figure Skating Team
Patricia Shelley Bushman, 2010

Indelible Images: An Illustrated History Of The 1961 U.S. World Figure Skating Team
Patricia Shelley Bushman, 2011

Frozen in Time: The Enduring Legacy of the 1961 U.S. Figure Skating Team
Nikki Nichols, 2008

Gundi Busch

Ice Skating
T.D. Richardson, 1956

Mein eiskaltes Leben
Gundi Busch, 2009, German language book

Günter Zöller

Chemnitz Eissterne
Martina Martin, 2010, German language book

Gustave Lussi

Figure Skating: A Celebration
Beverley Smith, 1994

Reader's Guide To Figure Skating's Hall of Fame
Benjamin T. Wright, Gregory Smith, U.S. Figure Skating Association, 1978

Lake Placid Figure Skating: A History
Christie Sausa, 2012

Minto: Skating Through Time, History of the Minto Skating Club 1904-2004
Janet B. Uren, 2004

Hana Mašková

Hana Mašková : příběh legendární krasobruslařky
Hana Kotíková, 2019, Czech language book

Hank Beatty

Reader's Guide To Figure Skating's Hall of Fame

Benjamin T. Wright, Gregory Smith, U.S. Figure Skating Association, 1978

Hanna Eigel

Traumfabrik auf dem Eis: Von der Wiener Eisrevue zu Holiday on Ice
Bernhard Hachleitner, Isabella Lechner, 2014, German language book

Hans Gerschwiler

Ice Skating
T.D. Richardson, 1956

Hayes Alan Jenkins

Figure Skating's Greatest Stars
Steve Milton, 2009

The Official Book of Figure Skating
U.S. Figure Skating Association, 1998

Reader's Guide To Figure Skating's Hall of Fame
Benjamin T. Wright, Gregory Smith, U.S. Figure Skating Association, 1978

The Skating Scene: Champions & Championships, The Fact Book of Skating
Arthur R. Goodfellow, 1981

Heaton R. Robertson

The First Twenty-Five Years of the United States Figure Skating Association 1921-1946
U.S. Figure Skating Association, 1946

Reader's Guide To Figure Skating's Hall of Fame
Benjamin T. Wright, Gregory Smith, U.S. Figure Skating Association, 1978

Hedy Stenuf

Die Eisparade: Meisterinnen auf Schlittschuhen, wie sie sind und wie sie wurden, Kampf um den Weltmeisterthron
Hans Saalbach, 1938, German language book

Henning Grenander

Ice Skating
T.D. Richardson, 1956

Henry Wainwright Howe

The First Twenty-Five Years of the United States Figure Skating Association 1921-1946
U.S. Figure Skating Association, 1946

Herbert Ramon Yglesias

Ice Skating
T.D. Richardson, 1956

Herma Szabo

Figure Skating's Greatest Stars
Steve Milton, 2009

150 Jahre Eiszeit: Die Grosse Geschichte des Wiener Eislauf-Vereines
Agnes Meisinger, 2017, German language book

Howard Nicholson

Reader's Guide To Figure Skating's Hall of Fame
Benjamin T. Wright, Gregory Smith, U.S. Figure Skating Association, 1978

Skaters' Cavalcade: Fifty Years of Skating
A.C.A. Wade, 1939

Igor Bobrin

Серия книг «Пара, в которой трое»- Читайте подробнее на
Natalia Bestemianova, Igor Bobrin, Andrei Bukin, 2010, updated and re-released in 2017, Russian language book

Ila Ray and Ray Hadley Jr.

Indelible Tracings: The Story of the 1961 U.S. World Figure Skating Team
Patricia Shelley Bushman, 2010

Indelible Images: An Illustrated History Of The 1961

U.S. World Figure Skating Team
Patricia Shelley Bushman, 2011

Frozen in Time: The Enduring Legacy of the 1961 U.S. Figure Skating Team
Nikki Nichols, 2008

Ilia Kulik

Skate Talk: Figure Skating In The Words Of The Stars
Steve Milton, 1998

Ilia Kulik: Prince Of Blades
Gregory Nicoll, 2000, children's/young adult book

Ice Stars: A Celebration of the Artistry, Beauty and Grace of the Ice-Skating World
Kevin Bursey, 1999

Inge Wischnewski

Die Pirouettenkönigin : Eiskunstlaufgeschichten rund um die Berliner Meistertrainerin Inge Wischnewski
Ingeborg Dittmann, Christine Stüber-Errath, 2010, German language book

Ingrid Wendl

Mein großer Bogen
Ingrid Wendl, 2002

Eis mit Stil: Eine Eisläuferin der Weltklasse - sie weiß

wovon sie spricht, wenn sie Wiener Eisgeschichten erzählt
Ingrid Wendl, 1979

Traumfabrik auf dem Eis: Von der Wiener Eisrevue zu Holiday on Ice
Bernhard Hachleitner, Isabella Lechner, 2014, German language book

Irina Lobacheva and Ilya Averbukh

Skate Talk: Figure Skating In The Words Of The Stars
Steve Milton, 1998

Ice Stars: A Celebration of the Artistry, Beauty and Grace of the Ice-Skating World
Kevin Bursey, 1999

Irina Moiseeva and Andrei Minenkov

Figure Skating's Greatest Stars
Steve Milton, 2009

Непревзойденные
Fedor Razzakov, 2014, Russian language book

Les Riches Heures du Patinage
Jean-Christophe Berlot, 2002, French language book

Irina Rodnina, Alexei Ulanov and Alexander Zaitsev

Figure Skating's Greatest Stars

Steve Milton, 2009

Ирина Роднина
Anatoly Tchaikovsky, 1977, Russian language book

Слезы на льду
Elena Vaitsekhovskaya, 2007, Russian language book

Слеза чемпионки
Irina Rodnina, 2014, Russian language book

Winners On The Ice (A Picture Life Book)
Frank Litsky, 1979, children's/young adult book

The Official Book of Figure Skating
U.S. Figure Skating Association, 1998

Les Riches Heures du Patinage
Jean-Christophe Berlot, 2002, French language book

Ирина Роднина — Александр Зайцев: Фотоочерк
Fitzcultura I Sport, 1981, Russian language book

Олимпийская орбита
Irina Rodnina, Alexander Zaitsev, 1984, Russian language book

Непревзойденные
Fedor Razzakov, 2014, Russian language book

Ice Stars: A Celebration of the Artistry, Beauty and Grace of the Ice-Skating World

Kevin Bursey, 1999

Irina Slutskaya

Figure Skating's Greatest Stars
Steve Milton, 2009

Figure Skating Champions
Steve Milton, Gérard Châtaigneau, 2002, children's/young adult book

Фигурное катание. Только звезды
Elena Vaitsekhovskaya, Alexander Wilf, 2008, Russian language book

Ice Stars: A Celebration of the Artistry, Beauty and Grace of the Ice-Skating World
Kevin Bursey, 1999

Irving Brokaw

Ice Skating
T.D. Richardson, 1956

Isabelle and Paul Duchesnay

Ice Skating: From Axels to Zambonis
Dan Gutman, 1995, children's/young adult book

Figure Skating: A Celebration
Beverley Smith, 1994

Ice Cream: Thirty of the Most Interesting Skaters in History
Toller Cranston, Martha Lowder Kimball, 2002

Figure Skating's Greatest Stars
Steve Milton, 2009

Talking Figure Skating: Behind The Scenes in the World's Most Glamourous Sport
Beverley Smith, 1997

Isabelle et Paul Duchesnay: Notre Passion
Isabelle and Paul Duchesnay, Martine Carret, 1992, French language book

Les Riches Heures du Patinage
Jean-Christophe Berlot, 2002, French language book

Minto: Skating Through Time, History of the Minto Skating Club 1904-2004
Janet B. Uren, 2004

Isabelle Brasseur and Lloyd Eisler

Skate Talk: Figure Skating In The Words Of The Stars
Steve Milton, 1998

Ice Skating: From Axels to Zambonis
Dan Gutman, 1995, children's/young adult book

Super Skaters: World Figure Skating Stars
Steve Milton, 1994, children's/young adult book

Brasseur & Eisler: The Professional Years
Isabelle Brasseur, Lloyd Eisler, Lynda Prouse, 1999

Brasseur & Eisler: to Catch a Dream
Isabelle Brasseur, Lloyd Eisler, Lynda Prouse, 1996

Isabelle Delobel and Olivier Schoenfelder

Figure Skating Today: The Next Wave of Stars
Steve Milton, Gérard Châtaigneau, 2007

Jack Dunn

Skaters' Cavalcade: Fifty Years of Skating
A.C.A. Wade, 1939

Jack Ferguson Page

Ice Skating
T.D. Richardson, 1956

Our Skating Heritage
Dennis L. Bird, 1979

Jackson Haines

Jackson Haines: The Skating King
Ryan Stevens, 2023

Slippery Shoes: A Fairy Tale About The American Skating King

John Mäki, 1994
Historical fiction – some accurate elements, some fictional

Figure Skating: A Celebration
Beverley Smith, 1994

Figure Skating's Greatest Stars
Steve Milton, 2009

The Golden Age of Canadian Figure Skating
David Young, 1984

Konståkningens 100-åriga historia - Utveckling, OS - VM - referater. Intervjuer och berättelser
Gunnar Bang, 1966, Swedish language book

Ice Skating
T.D. Richardson, 1956

Ice-Skating: A History
Nigel Brown, 1959

Reader's Guide To Figure Skating's Hall of Fame
Benjamin T. Wright, Gregory Smith, U.S. Figure Skating Association, 1978

The Skating Scene: Champions & Championships, The Fact Book of Skating
Arthur R. Goodfellow, 1981

Artistic Impressions: Figure Skating, Masculinity and the

Limits of Sport
Mary Louise Adams, 2011

Jacqueline du Bief

Thin Ice
Jacqueline du Bief, Eugénie Lorie, 1956

Jacques Gerschwiler

Reader's Guide To Figure Skating's Hall of Fame
Benjamin T. Wright, Gregory Smith, U.S. Figure Skating Association, 1978

Jaimee Eggleton

Talking Figure Skating: Behind The Scenes in the World's Most Glamourous Sport
Beverley Smith, 1997

James Drake Digby

Our Skating Heritage
Dennis L. Bird, 1979

Jamie Salé and David Pelletier

Figure Skating's Greatest Stars
Steve Milton, 2009

Figure Skating Champions
Steve Milton, Gérard Châtaigneau, 2002,

children's/young adult book

The Second Mark: Courage, Corruption, and the Battle for Olympic Gold
Joy Goodwin, 2007, though about the judging scandal at the 2002 Winter Olympic Games, this book has strong biographical elements

Gold on Ice: The Salé and Pelletier Story
Beverley Smith, 2002

Taking The Ice: Success Stories from the World of Canadian Figure Skating
PJ Kwong, 2010

Jan Hoffmann

Chemnitz Eissterne
Martina Martin, 2010, German language book

Janet Lynn
Figure Skating's Greatest Stars
Steve Milton, 2009

Figure Skating
Elizabeth van Steenwyk, 1976, children's/young adult book

The Wheel: Legacy Of Excellence
Janet Lynn, 2016, though primarily about The Wagon Wheel rink, this book has autobiographical elements

Janet Lynn: Figure Skating Star
Julian May, 1975, children's/young adult book

Janet Lynn, Sunshine On Ice
Linda Jacobs Altman, 1974, children's/young adult book

Peace + Love
Janet Lynn, Dean Merrill, 1973

Janet Lynn
Ann Morse, 1975, children's/young adult book

The Official Book of Figure Skating
U.S. Figure Skating Association, 1998

The Skating Scene: Champions & Championships, The Fact Book of Skating
Arthur R. Goodfellow, 1981

Les Riches Heures du Patinage
Jean-Christophe Berlot, 2002, French language book

Javier Fernández

Bailando el Hielo
Javier Fernández, 2016, Spanish language book

Jayne Torvill and Christopher Dean

Ice Skating: From Axels to Zambonis
Dan Gutman, 1995, children's/young adult book

Figure Skating: A Celebration
Beverley Smith, 1994

Ice Cream: Thirty of the Most Interesting Skaters in History
Toller Cranston, Martha Lowder Kimball, 2002

Figure Skating's Greatest Stars
Steve Milton, 2009

Super Skaters: World Figure Skating Stars
Steve Milton, 1994, children's/young adult book

Skate Talk: Figure Skating In The Words Of The Stars
Steve Milton, 1998

Skate: 100 Years Of Figure Skating
Steve Milton, Barbara McCutcheon, 1996

Partners: Jayne Torvill & Christopher Dean, Ice Dancing's Perfect Pair
Franny Shuker-Haines, 1995, children's/young adult book

Torvill and Dean: Fire on Ice
Jayne Torvill, Christopher Dean, Neil Wilson, 1994

Torvill & Dean: Our Life On Ice, The Autobiography
Jayne Torvill, Christopher Dean, 2014

Torvill & Dean
Jayne Torvill, Christopher Dean, John Hennessy, 1984

Torvill and Dean: The Full Story
Christopher Hilton, 1994

Torvill & Dean: Facing The Music, The Autobiography
(also released as Torvill & Dean: The Autobiography of
Ice Dancing's Greatest Stars
Jayne Torvill, Christopher Dean, John Man, 1996

Ice Stars: A Celebration of the Artistry, Beauty and
Grace of the Ice-Skating World
Kevin Bursey, 1999

The Official Book of Figure Skating
U.S. Figure Skating Association, 1998

BBC Book of Skating
Sandra Stevenson, 1984

Jean Westwood and Lawrence Demmy

Figure Skating's Greatest Stars
Steve Milton, 2009

Reader's Guide To Figure Skating's Hall of Fame
Benjamin T. Wright, Gregory Smith, U.S. Figure Skating
Association, 1978

Jeannette Altwegg

Earl's Court
Claude Langdon, 1953

Ice Skating
T.D. Richardson, 1956

Our Skating Heritage
Dennis L. Bird, 1979

Jeffrey Buttle

Figure Skating Today: The Next Wave of Stars
Steve Milton, Gérard Châtaigneau, 2007

Jenni Meno and Todd Sand

Skate Talk: Figure Skating In The Words Of The Stars
Steve Milton, 1998

Ice Stars: A Celebration of the Artistry, Beauty and Grace of the Ice-Skating World
Kevin Bursey, 1999

Jennifer Robinson

Talking Figure Skating: Behind The Scenes in the World's Most Glamourous Sport
Beverley Smith, 1997

Figure Skating Champions
Steve Milton, Gérard Châtaigneau, 2002, children's/young adult book

Jeremy Abbott

Skating Forward: Olympic Memories, Olympic Spirit
Joanne Vassallo Jamrosz, 2019

Jessica Dubé and Bryce Davison

Figure Skating Today: The Next Wave of Stars
Steve Milton, Gérard Châtaigneau, 2007

Taking The Ice: Success Stories from the World of Canadian Figure Skating
PJ Kwong, 2010

Jill Trenary

Time Of My Life: The Day I Skated For Gold
Jill Trenary, Dale Mitch, 1989

Jiřina Nekolová

Traumfabrik auf dem Eis: Von der Wiener Eisrevue zu Holiday on Ice
Bernhard Hachleitner, Isabella Lechner, 2014, German language book

Joan Haanappel

Op de schaats
H.J. Looman, 1961, Dutch language book

Joan Mitchell and Bobby Specht

Joan Mitchell: Lady Painter, A Life
Patricia Albers, 2011

Joannie Rochette

Figure Skating Today: The Next Wave of Stars
Steve Milton, Gérard Châtaigneau, 2007

Joannie Rochette: Ice Princess
Christine Dzidrums, Leah Rendon, Elizabeth Allison, 2010, children's/young adult book

Taking The Ice: Success Stories from the World of Canadian Figure Skating
PJ Kwong, 2010

John Curry

Ice Skating: From Axels to Zambonis
Dan Gutman, 1995, children's/young adult book

Figure Skating: A Celebration
Beverley Smith, 1994

Ice Cream: Thirty of the Most Interesting Skaters in History
Toller Cranston, Martha Lowder Kimball, 2002

Figure Skating's Greatest Stars
Steve Milton, 2009

Skate: 100 Years Of Figure Skating

Steve Milton, Barbara McCutcheon, 1996

Winners On The Ice (A Picture Life Book)
Frank Litsky, 1979, children's/young adult book

Black Ice: The Life And Death Of John Curry
Elva Oglanby, 1995, withdrawn after publication

John Curry
Keith Money, 1978

Alone: The Triumph And Tragedy Of John Curry
Bill Jones, 2014

Ice Stars: A Celebration of the Artistry, Beauty and Grace of the Ice-Skating World
Kevin Bursey, 1999

The Official Book of Figure Skating
U.S. Figure Skating Association, 1998

The Ice Skating Book
Robert Sheffield, Richard Woodward, 1980

Our Skating Heritage
Dennis L. Bird, 1979

Les Riches Heures du Patinage
Jean-Christophe Berlot, 2002, French language book

John Keiller Greig

Ice Skating
T.D. Richardson, 1956

John Knebli

Talking Figure Skating: Behind The Scenes in the World's Most Glamourous Sport
Beverley Smith, 1997

John Nicks

Skate Talk: Figure Skating In The Words Of The Stars
Steve Milton, 1998

Johnny Weir

Figure Skating Today: The Next Wave of Stars
Steve Milton, Gérard Châtaigneau, 2007

Welcome To My World
Johnny Weir, 2011

JoJo Starbuck and Ken Shelley

jojo STARbuck
JoJo Starbuck, Nina Ball, 1978

The Official Book of Figure Skating
U.S. Figure Skating Association, 1998

Josée Chouinard

Super Skaters: World Figure Skating Stars
Steve Milton, 1994, children's/young adult book

Skate Talk: Figure Skating In The Words Of The Stars
Steve Milton, 1998

All That Glitters
Josée Chouinard, Lynda Prouse, 2002

Joseph Chapman

Fifty Years Of Skating
Joseph Chapman, 1944

Joyce Hisey

Skate Talk: Figure Skating In The Words Of The Stars
Steve Milton, 1998

Jozef Sabovčík

Ice Cream: Thirty of the Most Interesting Skaters in History
Toller Cranston, Martha Lowder Kimball, 2002

Jumpin' Joe: The Jozef Sabovčík Story
Jozef Sabovčík, Lynda Prouse, 1998

Júlia Sebestyén

Figure Skating Today: The Next Wave of Stars
Steve Milton, Gérard Châtaigneau, 2007

Julia Soldatova

Ice Stars: A Celebration of the Artistry, Beauty and Grace of the Ice-Skating World
Kevin Bursey, 1999

Julianne Séguin

Une médaille à tout prix: Enquête sur les dérapages du patinage artistique au Québec
Julianne Séguin, Marie-Christine Noël, 2022, French language book

Julie Lynn Holmes

Skating With The World
Joanne Vassallo Jamrosz, 2014

June Markham, Doreen Denny and Courtney Jones

Our Skating Heritage
Dennis L. Bird, 1979

Figure Skating's Greatest Stars
Steve Milton, 2009

Around The Ice In Eighty Years: An Irreverent Memoir By An Accidental Champion
Courtney Jones, Helen Cox, 2021

The Official Book of Figure Skating

U.S. Figure Skating Association, 1998

Junko Yaginuma

アイスモデリスト
Junko Yaginuma, 2016, Japanese language book

Jutta Müller

Chemnitz Eissterne
Martina Martin, 2010, German language book

Jutta Müller: der schönste Sport der Welt; eine Eiskunstlauftrainerin erinnert sich
Manfred Hönel, 2008, German language book

Kanako Murakami

アイスモデリスト
Junko Yaginuma, 2012, Japanese language book

Karel Fajfr

Talking Figure Skating: Behind The Scenes in the World's Most Glamourous Sport
Beverley Smith, 1997

Karen Barber and Nicky Slater

Spice On Ice: The Story Of Britain's Ice Dancing Champions
Karen Barber, Nicky Slater, Sandra Stevenson, 1985

Karen Chen

Finding The Edge: My Life On The Ice
Karen Chen, 2018, children's/young adult book

Karen Magnussen

Figure Skating's Greatest Stars
Steve Milton, 2009

The Golden Age of Canadian Figure Skating
David Young, 1984

Karen: The Karen Magnussen Story
Karen Magnussen, Jeff Cross, 1973

Figure Skating
Elizabeth van Steenwyk, 1976, children's/young adult book

Taking The Ice: Success Stories from the World of Canadian Figure Skating
PJ Kwong, 2010

Karen Preston

Talking Figure Skating: Behind The Scenes in the World's Most Glamourous Sport
Beverley Smith, 1997

Karina Manta

On Top of Glass: My Stories As A Queer Girl in Figure Skating
Karina Manta, 2021

Karl Schäfer

Figure Skating's Greatest Stars
Steve Milton, 2009

Ice Skating
T.D. Richardson, 1956

Reader's Guide To Figure Skating's Hall of Fame
Benjamin T. Wright, Gregory Smith, U.S. Figure Skating Association, 1978

Katarina Witt

Ice Skating: From Axels to Zambonis
Dan Gutman, 1995, children's/young adult book

Ice Cream: Thirty of the Most Interesting Skaters in History
Toller Cranston, Martha Lowder Kimball, 2002

Figure Skating's Greatest Stars
Steve Milton, 2009

Katarina Witt
Wayne R. Coffey, 1992, children's/young adult book

Katarina Witt
Evelyn B. Kelly, 1999

Katarina: Eine Traumkarriere auf dem Eis
Volker Kluge, Manfred Hönel, 1988, German language book

Katarina Witt
Bernard Heimo, Félix Clément, 1988

Only With Passion: Figure Skating's Most Winning Champion on Competition and Life
Katarina Witt, E.M. Swift, 2007

Gesund und fit mit Kati Witt: So werden auch Sie fit mit dem Programm der erfolgreichsten (Healthy and Fit with Kati Witt)
Katarina Witt, 2016, German language book, fitness book with autobiographical elements

So viel Leben
Katarina Witt, 2015, German language book

Meine Jahre zwischen Pflicht und Kür
Katarina Witt, C. Bertelsmann, 1994, German language book

Mes Dossier Secrets: Une star du patinage face à la Stasi
Danielle de Leusse, 1994, French language book

Ice Stars: A Celebration of the Artistry, Beauty and Grace of the Ice-Skating World

Kevin Bursey, 1999

The Official Book of Figure Skating
U.S. Figure Skating Association, 1998

Rivals: Legendary Matchups That Made Sports History
David Kenneth Wiggins, Pierre R. Rodgers, 2010

Chemnitz Eissterne
Martina Martin, 2010, German language book

Katherine Healy

A Very Young Skater
Jill Krementz, 1979, children's/young adult book

Keri Blakinger

Corrections in Ink: A Memoir
Keri Blakinger, 2022

Kerry Leitch

Skate Talk: Figure Skating In The Words Of The Stars
Steve Milton, 1998

Kiira Korpi

Figure Skating Today: The Next Wave of Stars
Steve Milton, Gérard Châtaigneau, 2007

Kiira Korpi: Surviving The Ruthless World Of

Competitive Figure Skating
Kiira Korpi, Jere Nurminen, 2022

Kimmie Meissner

Figure Skating's Greatest Stars
Steve Milton, 2009

Figure Skating Today: The Next Wave of Stars
Steve Milton, Gérard Châtaigneau, 2007

Kitty and Peter Carruthers

The Official Book of Figure Skating
U.S. Figure Skating Association, 1998

Kristi Yamaguchi

Ice Skating: From Axels to Zambonis
Dan Gutman, 1995, children's/young adult book

Figure Skating's Greatest Stars
Steve Milton, 2009

Super Skaters: World Figure Skating Stars
Steve Milton, 1994, children's/young adult book

Asian Americans of Achievement: Kristi Yamaguchi
Judy L. Hasday, 2007, children's/young adult book

Kristi Yamaguchi: Artist On Ice
Shiobhan Donohue, 1994, children's/young adult book

Kristi Yamaguchi
Sam Wellman, 1999, children's/young adult book

Kristi Yamaguchi
Richard Rambeck, 1994, children's/young adult book

Always Dream
Kristi Yamaguchi, Greg Brown, 1998

Kristi Yamaguchi
Elaine A. Kule, 2006, children's/young adult book

Ice Stars: A Celebration of the Artistry, Beauty and Grace of the Ice-Skating World
Kevin Bursey, 1999

The Official Book of Figure Skating
U.S. Figure Skating Association, 1998

Kristy Sargeant and Kris Wirtz

Talking Figure Skating: Behind The Scenes in the World's Most Glamourous Sport
Beverley Smith, 1997

Skate Talk: Figure Skating In The Words Of The Stars
Steve Milton, 1998

Kurt Browning

Ice Skating: From Axels to Zambonis

Dan Gutman, 1995, children's/young adult book

Figure Skating: A Celebration
Beverley Smith, 1994

Ice Cream: Thirty of the Most Interesting Skaters in History
Toller Cranston, Martha Lowder Kimball, 2002

Figure Skating's Greatest Stars
Steve Milton, 2009

Talking Figure Skating: Behind The Scenes in the World's Most Glamourous Sport
Beverley Smith, 1997

Super Skaters: World Figure Skating Stars
Steve Milton, 1994, children's/young adult book

Skate Talk: Figure Skating In The Words Of The Stars
Steve Milton, 1998

Kurt: Forcing The Edge
Kurt Browning, Neil Stevens, 1991

Ice Stars: A Celebration of the Artistry, Beauty and Grace of the Ice-Skating World
Kevin Bursey, 1999

The Official Book of Figure Skating
U.S. Figure Skating Association, 1998

Taking The Ice: Success Stories from the World of Canadian Figure Skating
PJ Kwong, 2010

Kyoko Ina, Jason Dungjen and John Zimmerman

Skate Talk: Figure Skating In The Words Of The Stars
Steve Milton, 1998

The Official Book of Figure Skating
U.S. Figure Skating Association, 1998

Figure Skating Champions
Steve Milton, Gérard Châtaigneau, 2002, children's/young adult book

Larry Holliday

The Larry Holliday Story: Someone You Should Know
Norma Jean, 2009

Laurence Owen

Indelible Tracings: The Story of the 1961 U.S. World Figure Skating Team
Patricia Shelley Bushman, 2010

Indelible Images: An Illustrated History Of The 1961 U.S. World Figure Skating Team
Patricia Shelley Bushman, 2011

Frozen in Time: The Enduring Legacy of the 1961 U.S.

Figure Skating Team
Nikki Nichols, 2008

Laurent Tobel

Ice Cream: Thirty of the Most Interesting Skaters in History
Toller Cranston, Martha Lowder Kimball, 2002

Ice Stars: A Celebration of the Artistry, Beauty and Grace of the Ice-Skating World
Kevin Bursey, 1999

Laurie and Bill Hickox

Indelible Tracings: The Story of the 1961 U.S. World Figure Skating Team
Patricia Shelley Bushman, 2010

Indelible Images: An Illustrated History Of The 1961 U.S. World Figure Skating Team
Patricia Shelley Bushman, 2011

Frozen in Time: The Enduring Legacy of the 1961 U.S. Figure Skating Team
Nikki Nichols, 2008

Leonore Kay

Talking Figure Skating: Behind The Scenes in the World's Most Glamourous Sport
Beverley Smith, 1997

Lili Kronberger

Figure Skating's Greatest Stars
Steve Milton, 2009

Lili Scholz and Otto Kaiser

Ice Skating
T.D. Richardson, 1956

Linda Fratianne

Figure Skating: A Celebration
Beverley Smith, 1994

Figure Skating's Greatest Stars
Steve Milton, 2009

The Official Book of Figure Skating
U.S. Figure Skating Association, 1998

Lisa-Marie Allen

Skating With The World
Joanne Vassallo Jamrosz, 2014

Little Winners: Inside The World of Child Sports
Emily Greenspan, 1983

Lori Nichol

Talking Figure Skating: Behind The Scenes in the
World's Most Glamourous Sport
Beverley Smith, 1997

Skate Talk: Figure Skating In The Words Of The Stars
Steve Milton, 1998

Taking The Ice: Success Stories from the World of
Canadian Figure Skating
PJ Kwong, 2010

Louis and Marijane Stong

Talking Figure Skating: Behind The Scenes in the
World's Most Glamourous Sport
Beverley Smith, 1997

Reflections on the CFSA 1887-1990: A History of the
Canadian Figure Skating Association
Teresa Moore, Canadian Figure Skating Association,
1993

The Golden Age of Canadian Figure Skating
David Young, 1984

Louise and Harold Hartshorne

Indelible Tracings: The Story of the 1961 U.S. World
Figure Skating Team
Patricia Shelley Bushman, 2010

Indelible Images: An Illustrated History Of The 1961

U.S. World Figure Skating Team
Patricia Shelley Bushman, 2011

Frozen in Time: The Enduring Legacy of the 1961 U.S. Figure Skating Team
Nikki Nichols, 2008

Lu Chen

Figure Skating: A Celebration
Beverley Smith, 1994

Super Skaters: World Figure Skating Stars
Steve Milton, 1994, children's/young adult book

A Year In Figure Skating
Beverley Smith, 1996

Ice Stars: A Celebration of the Artistry, Beauty and Grace of the Ice-Skating World
Kevin Bursey, 1999

Les Riches Heures du Patinage
Jean-Christophe Berlot, 2002, French language book

Lucinda Ruh

Ice Cream: Thirty of the Most Interesting Skaters in History
Toller Cranston, Martha Lowder Kimball, 2002

Skate Talk: Figure Skating In The Words Of The Stars

Steve Milton, 1998

Frozen Teardrop: The Tragedy and Triumph of Figure Skating's "Queen of Spin"
Lucinda Ruh, 2012

Ice Stars: A Celebration of the Artistry, Beauty and Grace of the Ice-Skating World
Kevin Bursey, 1999

Ludmila and Oleg Protopopov

Figure Skating: A Celebration
Beverley Smith, 1994

Ice Cream: Thirty of the Most Interesting Skaters in History
Toller Cranston, Martha Lowder Kimball, 2002

Figure Skating's Greatest Stars
Steve Milton, 2009

Ледовая симфония
Anatoly Shelukhin, 1969, Russian language book

Золотые коньки с бриллиантами
Ludmila Protopopov, Oleg Protopopov, 1971, Russian language book

Слезы на льду
Elena Vaitsekhovskaya, 2007, Russian language book

Непревзойденные
Fedor Razzakov, 2014, Russian language book

Ice Stars: A Celebration of the Artistry, Beauty and Grace of the Ice-Skating World
Kevin Bursey, 1999

The Official Book of Figure Skating
U.S. Figure Skating Association, 1998

Reader's Guide To Figure Skating's Hall of Fame
Benjamin T. Wright, Gregory Smith, U.S. Figure Skating Association, 1978

Les Riches Heures du Patinage
Jean-Christophe Berlot, 2002, French language book

Lynn Nightingale

Skate Talk: Figure Skating In The Words Of The Stars
Steve Milton, 1998

Minto: Skating Through Time, History of the Minto Skating Club 1904-2004
Janet B. Uren, 2004

Lyudmila Pakhomova and Aleksandr Gorshkov

Монолог после аплодисментов
Lyudmila Pakhomova, 1977, Russian language book

Ice Cream: Thirty of the Most Interesting Skaters in

History
Toller Cranston, Martha Lowder Kimball, 2002

Figure Skating's Greatest Stars
Steve Milton, 2009

И вечно музыка звучит…
Aleksandr Gorshkov, 2006, Russian language book

Непревзойдённые
Fedor Razzakov, 2014, Russian language book

Ice Stars: A Celebration of the Artistry, Beauty and Grace of the Ice-Skating World
Kevin Bursey, 1999

Mabel Fairbanks

Black Women in America
Darlene Clark Hine, 2005

Marvellous Mabel: Figure Skating Superstar
Crystal Hubbard, 2022, children's/young adult book

Ice Breaker: How Mabel Fairbanks Changed Figure Skating
Rose Viña, Claire Almon, 2019, children's/young adult book

Madge and Edgar Syers

Ice Skating

T.D. Richardson, 1956

Our Skating Heritage
Dennis L. Bird, 1979

Ice Skating: From Axels to Zambonis
Dan Gutman, 1995, children's/young adult book

Figure Skating: A Celebration
Beverley Smith, 1994

The Official Book of Figure Skating
U.S. Figure Skating Association, 1998

Maj-Britt Röningberg

Vintergatan
Maj-Britt Röningberg, 1996, Swedish language book

Mandy Wötzel and Ingo Steuer

Eiszeiten: Vom Ehrgeiz getrieben
Ingo Steuer, Sophie Micheel, 2014

Skate Talk: Figure Skating In The Words Of The Stars
Steve Milton, 1998

Ice Stars: A Celebration of the Artistry, Beauty and Grace of the Ice-Skating World
Kevin Bursey, 1999

Chemnitz Eissterne

Martina Martin, 2010, German language book

Meine Sohn Ingo Steuer
Paul G. Steuer, 2008, German language book

Manfred Schnelldorfer

Triumph auf dem Eis
Heinz Maegerlein, 1964, German language book

Manon Perron

Taking The Ice: Success Stories from the World of Canadian Figure Skating
PJ Kwong, 2010

Mao Asada

Figure Skating Today: The Next Wave of Stars
Steve Milton, Gérard Châtaigneau, 2007

浅田真央 100 の言葉
Fusosha, 2020, Japanese language book

夢をかなえる力—私がスケートから学んだこと—
Mao Asada, Shinshokan, 2020, Japanese language book

浅田真央 オフィシャルフォトエッセイ また、この場所で
Shueisha, 2018, Japanese language photo book

浅田真央 私のスケート人生
Shinshokan, 2017, Japanese language book

浅田真央 希望の軌跡
Shinshokan, 2017, Japanese language book

浅田真央 夢の軌跡〜ドリームのきせき〜
Shinshokan, 2013, Japanese language book

浅田真央 age 18-20
Bungei Shunju, 2013, Japanese language book

浅田真央 そして、その瞬間へ
Gakken Marketing, 2013, Japanese language book

浅田真央 美しく舞う言葉
East Press, 2012, Japanese language book

浅田真央 Book for Charity
Gakken Education Publishing, 2011, Japanese language book

浅田真央、20 歳への階段
Bungei Shunju, 2011, Japanese language book

浅田真央 さらなる高みへ
Gakken Education Publishing, 2011, Japanese language book

浅田真央物語 Princess Mao
Kadokawa Shoten, 2010, Japanese language book

浅田真央 POWER & BEAUTY
Shogakukan, 2010, Japanese language book

浅田真央公式写真集 MAO
Tokuma Shoten, 2010, Japanese language photo book

浅田真央 奇跡(ミラクル)
Shinshokan, 2010, Japanese language photo book,

真央らしく
Asahi Shimbun Publishing, 2009, , Japanese language book

浅田真央 age 15-17
Bungei Shunju, 2009, compilation of 3 previous books, Japanese language book

浅田真央、18歳
Bungei Shunju, 2009, Japanese language book

浅田真央、17歳
Bungei Shunju, 2008, Japanese language book

浅田真央、16歳
Bungei Shunju, 2007, Japanese language book

浅田真央、15歳
Bungei Shunju, 2006, Japanese language book

アイスモデリスト
Junko Yaginuma, 2012, Japanese language book

Marg and Bruce Hyland

Skate Talk: Figure Skating In The Words Of The Stars
Steve Milton, 1998

Margaret Bland Jameson

The Long Day 1883-1983
Margaret Bland Jameson, 1983

Maria and Otto Jelinek

The Golden Age of Canadian Figure Skating
David Young, 1984

On Thin Ice
Henry Jelinek, Ann Pinchot, 1978

Maria Butyrskaya

Фигурное катание. Только звезды
Elena Vaitsekhovskaya, Alexander Wilf, 2008, Russian language book

Ice Stars: A Celebration of the Artistry, Beauty and Grace of the Ice-Skating World
Kevin Bursey, 1999

Maribel Vinson Owen

Indelible Tracings: The Story of the 1961 U.S. World Figure Skating Team
Patricia Shelley Bushman, 2010

Indelible Images: An Illustrated History Of The 1961
U.S. World Figure Skating Team
Patricia Shelley Bushman, 2011

Frozen in Time: The Enduring Legacy of the 1961 U.S.
Figure Skating Team
Nikki Nichols, 2008

Maribel Y. Vinson's Advanced Figure Skating
Maribel Vinson Owen, 1940, like her other books,
primarily instructional but the latter part of this book is
autobiographical

Reader's Guide To Figure Skating's Hall of Fame
Benjamin T. Wright, Gregory Smith, U.S. Figure Skating
Association, 1978

Skaters' Cavalcade: Fifty Years of Skating
A.C.A. Wade, 1939

Maribel Y. Owen Jr. and Dudley Richards

Indelible Tracings: The Story of the 1961 U.S. World
Figure Skating Team
Patricia Shelley Bushman, 2010

Indelible Images: An Illustrated History Of The 1961
U.S. World Figure Skating Team
Patricia Shelley Bushman, 2011

Frozen in Time: The Enduring Legacy of the 1961 U.S.
Figure Skating Team

Nikki Nichols, 2008

Marie-France Dubreuil and Patrice Lauzon

Figure Skating Today: The Next Wave of Stars
Steve Milton, Gérard Châtaigneau, 2007

Taking The Ice: Success Stories from the World of Canadian Figure Skating
PJ Kwong, 2010

Marika Kilius and Hans-Jürgen Bäumler

Kilius-Bäumler: Traumpaar auf dem Eis
Heinz Knopp, 1964, German language book

Triumph auf dem Eis
Heinz Maegerlein, 1964, German language book

Traumfabrik auf dem Eis: Von der Wiener Eisrevue zu Holiday on Ice
Bernhard Hachleitner, Isabella Lechner, 2014, German language book

Weltmeister auf dem Eis: Kilius/Bäumler
Roderich Menzel, 1963, German language book

Marina Anissina and Gwendal Peizerat

Je ne suis pas de glace
Marina Anissina, 2007, French language book

Figure Skating Champions
Steve Milton, Gérard Châtaigneau, 2002, children's/young adult book

D'or et le fou
Marina Anissina, Gwendal Peizerat, 2002, French language book

Ice Stars: A Celebration of the Artistry, Beauty and Grace of the Ice-Skating World
Kevin Bursey, 1999

Marina Klimova and Sergei Ponomarenko

Figure Skating's Greatest Stars
Steve Milton, 2009

Marina Zoueva

Talking Figure Skating: Behind The Scenes in the World's Most Glamourous Sport
Beverley Smith, 1997

Skate Talk: Figure Skating In The Words Of The Stars
Steve Milton, 1998

Mary Rose Thacker

The Girl and The Game: A History of Women's Sport in Canada
Margaret Anne Hall, 2002

Maxi Herber and Ernst Baier

Figure Skating's Greatest Stars
Steve Milton, 2009

Ice Skating
T.D. Richardson, 1956

Maxi and Ernst Baier erzählen
Benno Wellman, 1951, German language book

Die Eisparade: Meisterinnen auf Schlittschuhen, wie sie sind und wie sie wurden, Kampf um den Weltmeisterthron
Hans Saalbach, 1938, German language book

Maya Usova and Alexandr Zhulin

Танцы на льду жизни. «Я знаю о любви все…»
Alexandr Zhulin, 2022, Russian language book

Meagan Duhamel and Eric Radford

Soulmates On Ice: From Hometown Glory To The Top Of The Podium
Meagan Duhamel, Eric Radford, Laura E. Young, 2018

Megan Taylor

Earl's Court
Claude Langdon, 1953

Die Eisparade: Meisterinnen auf Schlittschuhen, wie sie sind und wie sie wurden, Kampf um den Weltmeisterthron
Hans Saalbach, 1938, German language book

Ice Skating
T.D. Richardson, 1956

Skaters' Cavalcade: Fifty Years of Skating
A.C.A. Wade, 1939

Britain's Olympic Women: A History
Jean Williams, 2021

Our Skating Heritage
Dennis L. Bird, 1979

Melville Rogers

Minto: Skating Through Time, History of the Minto Skating Club 1904-2004
Janet B. Uren, 2004

Meryl Davis and Charlie White

Figure Skating Today: The Next Wave of Stars
Steve Milton, Gérard Châtaigneau, 2007

Michael Kirby

Figure Skating to Fancy Skating: Memoirs of the Life of Sonja Henie

Michael Kirby, 2000, though primarily about Sonja Henie this book is definitely autobiographical as well

Michael Shmerkin

A Year In Figure Skating
Beverley Smith, 1996

Michael Weiss

Figure Skating Champions
Steve Milton, Gérard Châtaigneau, 2002, children's/young adult book

Ice Stars: A Celebration of the Artistry, Beauty and Grace of the Ice-Skating World
Kevin Bursey, 1999

Michelle Kwan

Ice Skating: From Axels to Zambonis
Dan Gutman, 1995, children's/young adult book

Figure Skating: A Celebration
Beverley Smith, 1994

Figure Skating's Greatest Stars
Steve Milton, 2009

Talking Figure Skating: Behind The Scenes in the World's Most Glamourous Sport
Beverley Smith, 1997

Skate Talk: Figure Skating In The Words Of The Stars
Steve Milton, 1998

Figure Skating Champions
Steve Milton, Gérard Châtaigneau, 2002,
children's/young adult book

Michelle Kwan
Stephanie Cham, 2020, children's/young adult book

Michelle Kwan (Women Who Win)
Sherry Beck Paprocki, 2000, children's/young adult book

Asian Americans Of Achievement: Michelle Kwan
Rachel A. Koestler-Grack, 2007, children's/young adult book

Michelle Kwan: Champion On Ice
Kimberly Gatto, 1998, children's/young adult book

Michelle Kwan
Rosemary Wallner, 2001, children's/young adult book

Michelle Kwan: Quest For Gold
Mark Stewart, Mike Kennedy, 2002

Michelle Kwan: My Book Of Memories, A Photo Diary
Michelle Kwan, 1998, children's/young adult book

Michelle Kwan (Real Life-Reader Biography)

John Albert Torres, 2000, children's/young adult book

Michelle Kwan: Figure Skater
Todd Peterson, 2006, children's/young adult book

Born To Skate: The Michelle Kwan Story
Edward Z. Epstein, 1997

Michelle Kwan: My Story, Heart Of A Champion
Michelle Kwan, Laura James, 1998

Michelle Kwan: Skating From The Wind
Linda Shaughnessy, 1998, children's/young adult book

Tara And Michelle: The Road To Gold
Wendy Daly, 1997, children's/young adult book

Skating For The Gold: Michelle Kwan & Tara Lipinski
Chip Lovitt, 1997, children's/young adult book

Ice Stars: A Celebration of the Artistry, Beauty and Grace of the Ice-Skating World
Kevin Bursey, 1999

The Official Book of Figure Skating
U.S. Figure Skating Association, 1998

Midori Ito

Ice Skating: From Axels to Zambonis
Dan Gutman, 1995, children's/young adult book

Ice Cream: Thirty of the Most Interesting Skaters in History
Toller Cranston, Martha Lowder Kimball, 2002

Figure Skating's Greatest Stars
Steve Milton, 2009

氷上の宝石：伊藤みどり写真集
Teruo Saegusa, Naoko Kojima, Masaharu Sugawara, 1993, Japanese language book

タイム・パッセージ：時間旅行
Midori Ito, Naoko Yoshida, Teruo Saegusa, 1993, Japanese language book

Miki Ando

My Way~安藤美姫写真集（
Miki Ando, Shueisha, 2014, Japanese language photo book

空に向かって
Miki Ando, Fusosha, 2010, Japanese language book

安藤美姫物語-I believe-
Miki Ando, Kodansha, 2009, Japanese language book

氷上のアーティストたち: 日本フィギュアスケートトリノを目指す銀盤の選手たち
Junko Yaginuma, 2005, Japanese language book

Figure Skating Today: The Next Wave of Stars

Steve Milton, Gérard Châtaigneau, 2007

Minoru Sano

氷上より愛をこめて　愛・夢・スケーター
Minoru Sano, 1982, Japanese language book

Montgomery Wilson

Reader's Guide To Figure Skating's Hall of Fame
Benjamin T. Wright, Gregory Smith, U.S. Figure Skating Association, 1978

Morris Chalfen

The Skating Scene: Champions & Championships, The Fact Book of Skating
Arthur R. Goodfellow, 1981

Nancy Kerrigan

Ice Skating: From Axels to Zambonis
Dan Gutman, 1995, children's/young adult book

Ice Cream: Thirty of the Most Interesting Skaters in History
Toller Cranston, Martha Lowder Kimball, 2002

Super Skaters: World Figure Skating Stars
Steve Milton, 1994, children's/young adult book

Skate: 100 Years Of Figure Skating

Steve Milton, Barbara McCutcheon, 1996

Women on Ice: Feminist Responses to the Tonya Harding/Nancy Kerrigan Spectacle
Cynthia Baughman, 1995

Nancy Kerrigan: In My Own Words
Nancy Kerrigan, Steve Woodward, 1996, children's/young adult book

Nancy Kerrigan, Olympic Figure Skater
Bob Italia, 1994, children's/young adult book

Nancy Kerrigan
Paula Edelson, 1999, children's/young adult book

Nancy Kerrigan: Heart Of A Champion
Mikki Morrisette, 1994, children's/young adult book

The Kerrigan Courage: Nancy's Story
Randi Ricefield, 1994

Ice Stars: A Celebration of the Artistry, Beauty and Grace of the Ice-Skating World
Kevin Bursey, 1999

The Official Book of Figure Skating
U.S. Figure Skating Association, 1998

Les Riches Heures du Patinage
Jean-Christophe Berlot, 2002, French language book

Naomi Lang and Peter Tchernyshev

Figure Skating Champions
Steve Milton, Gérard Châtaigneau, 2002,
children's/young adult book

Naomi Nari Nam and Themistocles Leftheris

Figure Skating Today: The Next Wave of Stars
Steve Milton, Gérard Châtaigneau, 2007

Natalia Bestemianova and Andrei Bukin

Figure Skating's Greatest Stars
Steve Milton, 2009

Серия книг «Пара, в которой трое»- Читайте подробнее на
Natalia Bestemianova, Igor Bobrin, Andrei Bukin, 2010, updated and re-released in 2017, Russian language book

Непревзойденные
Fedor Razzakov, 2014, Russian language book

Natalia Dubova

Skate Talk: Figure Skating In The Words Of The Stars
Steve Milton, 1998

Так сказал тренер
Natalia Dubova, 2021, Russian language book

Natalia Mishkutenok and Artur Dmitriev

Figure Skating's Greatest Stars
Steve Milton, 2009

Natalie and Wayne Seybold

Skating With The World
Joanne Vassallo Jamrosz, 2014

Nathalie Péchalat and Fabian Bourzat

Les bénéfices du doute
Nathalie Péchalat, 2020, French language book

Nathan Chen

One Jump At A Time: My Story
Nathan Chen, Alice Park, 2022

Nicole Bobek

Ice Skating: From Axels to Zambonis
Dan Gutman, 1995, children's/young adult book

Nicole Bobek
Veda Boyd Jones, 1999, children's/young adult book

Ice Stars: A Celebration of the Artistry, Beauty and Grace of the Ice-Skating World
Kevin Bursey, 1999

Nigel Stephens

Minto: Skating Through Time, History of the Minto Skating Club 1904-2004
Janet B. Uren, 2004

Nikolay Panin-Kolomenkin

Волшебная восьмерка
Anatoly Tchaikovsky, 1978, Russian language book

Figure Skating Today: The Next Wave of Stars
Steve Milton, Gérard Châtaigneau, 2007

Nobunari Oda

氷上のアーティストたち: 日本フィギュアスケートトリノを目指す銀盤の選手たち
Junko Yaginuma, 2005

フィギュアほど泣けるスポーツはない!
Nobunari Oda, 2008, Japanese language book

Nobuo Sato

Figure Skating: A Celebration
Beverley Smith, 1994

諦めない力 フィギュアスケートから教えられたこと
Nobuo Sato, 2018, Japanese language book

Norah McCarthy

The Girl and The Game: A History of Women's Sport in Canada
Margaret Anne Hall, 2002

Norval Baptie

The Golden Age of Canadian Figure Skating
David Young, 1984

The Skating Scene: Champions & Championships, The Fact Book of Skating
Arthur R. Goodfellow, 1981

Oksana Baiul

Ice Skating: From Axels to Zambonis
Dan Gutman, 1995, children's/young adult book

Ice Cream: Thirty of the Most Interesting Skaters in History
Toller Cranston, Martha Lowder Kimball, 2002

Super Skaters: World Figure Skating Stars
Steve Milton, 1994, children's/young adult book

Skate: 100 Years Of Figure Skating
Steve Milton, Barbara McCutcheon, 1996

Secrets Of Skating
Oksana Baiul, 1997

Oksana: My Own Story
Oksana Baiul, Heather Alexander, 1997,
children's/young adult book

Oksana Baiul: Rhapsody On Ice
Linda Shaughnessy, 1998, children's/young adult book

Oksana Baiul
Richard Rambeck, 1996, children's/young adult book

Oksana Baiul
Lonnie Hull DuPont, 1999, children's/young adult book

Ice Stars: A Celebration of the Artistry, Beauty and
Grace of the Ice-Skating World
Kevin Bursey, 1999

Oksana Domnina and Maxim Shabalin

Figure Skating Today: The Next Wave of Stars
Steve Milton, Gérard Châtaigneau, 2007

Oksana Grishuk and Evgeni Platov

Les Riches Heures du Patinage
Jean-Christophe Berlot, 2002, French language book

Figure Skating's Greatest Stars
Steve Milton, 2009

Слезы на льду
Elena Vaitsekhovskaya, 2007, Russian language book

Ice Stars: A Celebration of the Artistry, Beauty and Grace of the Ice-Skating World
Kevin Bursey, 1999

Oksana Kazakova and Artur Dmitriev

Ice Stars: A Celebration of the Artistry, Beauty and Grace of the Ice-Skating World
Kevin Bursey, 1999

Ondrej Nepela

Najlepší!: skutočný príbeh najúspešnejšieho športovca 20. storočia Ondreja Nepelu a jeho trénerky Hildy Múdrej
Eva Bacigalová, 2017, Slovak language book

Ked

Ottavio Cinquanta

Skate Talk: Figure Skating In The Words Of The Stars
Steve Milton, 1998

Patricia and Robert Dineen

Indelible Tracings: The Story of the 1961 U.S. World Figure Skating Team
Patricia Shelley Bushman, 2010

Indelible Images: An Illustrated History Of The 1961 U.S. World Figure Skating Team
Patricia Shelley Bushman, 2011

Frozen in Time: The Enduring Legacy of the 1961 U.S. Figure Skating Team
Nikki Nichols, 2008

Patrick Chan

Figure Skating Today: The Next Wave of Stars
Steve Milton, Gérard Châtaigneau, 2007

Patrick Chan
Jennifer Sutoski, 2016, children's/young adult book

Paul Wirtz

Talking Figure Skating: Behind The Scenes in the World's Most Glamourous Sport
Beverley Smith, 1997

Paul Wylie

Ice Skating: From Axels to Zambonis
Dan Gutman, 1995, children's/young adult book

Finding God At Harvard - Spiritual Journeys of Thinking Christians
Kelly Monroe, 1996, religious book that contains an essay by Paul Wylie

The Official Book of Figure Skating
U.S. Figure Skating Association, 1998

Peggy Fleming

Ice Skating: From Axels to Zambonis
Dan Gutman, 1995, children's/young adult book

Ice Cream: Thirty of the Most Interesting Skaters in History
Toller Cranston, Martha Lowder Kimball, 2002

Figure Skating's Greatest Stars
Steve Milton, 2009

Peggy Fleming: Cameo Of A Champion
Elizabeth van Steenwyk, 1978, children's/young adult book

Winners On The Ice (A Picture Life Book)
Frank Litsky, 1979, children's/young adult book

The Long Program: Skating Toward's Life's Victories
Peggy Fleming, Peter Kaminsky, 1999

Figure Skating
Elizabeth van Steenwyk, 1976, children's/young adult book

Ice Stars: A Celebration of the Artistry, Beauty and Grace of the Ice-Skating World
Kevin Bursey, 1999

The Official Book of Figure Skating
U.S. Figure Skating Association, 1998

Reader's Guide To Figure Skating's Hall of Fame
Benjamin T. Wright, Gregory Smith, U.S. Figure Skating Association, 1978

Petra Burka

Figure Skating: A Celebration
Beverley Smith, 1994

Figure Skating's Greatest Stars
Steve Milton, 2009

The Golden Age of Canadian Figure Skating
David Young, 1984

Taking The Ice: Success Stories from the World of Canadian Figure Skating

PJ Kwong, 2010

Phil Taylor

Skaters' Cavalcade: Fifty Years of Skating
A.C.A. Wade, 1939

Philippe Candeloro

Ice Cream: Thirty of the Most Interesting Skaters in History
Toller Cranston, Martha Lowder Kimball, 2002

Super Skaters: World Figure Skating Stars
Steve Milton, 1994, children's/young adult book

Skate Talk: Figure Skating In The Words Of The Stars
Steve Milton, 1998

Candeloro: Prince de la Glace
Patrick Mahé, 1995, French language book

Candel: Rebelle et fidèle
Philippe Candeloro, A. Leblond, 2005, French language book

Figure Libre
Philippe Candeloro, 2012, French language book

Ice Stars: A Celebration of the Artistry, Beauty and Grace of the Ice-Skating World
Kevin Bursey, 1999

Phyllis and James Henry Johnson

Ice Skating
T.D. Richardson, 1956

Pierrette Paquin Devine

Minto: Skating Through Time, History of the Minto Skating Club 1904-2004
Janet B. Uren, 2004

Qing Pang and Jian Tong

Figure Skating Today: The Next Wave of Stars
Steve Milton, Gérard Châtaigneau, 2007

Rachael Flatt

Skating With The World
Joanne Vassallo Jamrosz, 2014

Radka Kovaříková and René Novotný

Figure Skating: A Celebration
Beverley Smith, 1994

Reginald J. Wilkie

Reader's Guide To Figure Skating's Hall of Fame
Benjamin T. Wright, Gregory Smith, U.S. Figure Skating Association, 1978

Our Skating Heritage
Dennis L. Bird, 1979

Regine Heitzer

Traumfabrik auf dem Eis: Von der Wiener Eisrevue zu Holiday on Ice
Bernhard Hachleitner, Isabella Lechner, 2014, German language book

Rhode Lee Michelson

Indelible Tracings: The Story of the 1961 U.S. World Figure Skating Team
Patricia Shelley Bushman, 2010

Indelible Images: An Illustrated History Of The 1961 U.S. World Figure Skating Team
Patricia Shelley Bushman, 2011

Frozen in Time: The Enduring Legacy of the 1961 U.S. Figure Skating Team
Nikki Nichols, 2008

Ria Baran and Paul Falk

Ice Skating
T.D. Richardson, 1956

Robin Cousins

Figure Skating: A Celebration
Beverley Smith, 1994

Ice Cream: Thirty of the Most Interesting Skaters in History
Toller Cranston, Martha Lowder Kimball, 2002

Figure Skating's Greatest Stars
Steve Milton, 2009

Skate Talk: Figure Skating In The Words Of The Stars
Steve Milton, 1998

Robin Cousins: Skating For Gold
Robin Cousins, Howard Bass, 1980

Robin Cousins: The Authorized Biography
Robin Cousins, Martha Lowder Kimball, 1998

Ice Stars: A Celebration of the Artistry, Beauty and Grace of the Ice-Skating World
Kevin Bursey, 1999

Roger Turner

Polished Steel
Roger Turner, 1984

Romy Kermer and Rolf Oesterreich

Chemnitz Eissterne
Martina Martin, 2010, German language book

Rosalynn Sumners

The Official Book of Figure Skating
U.S. Figure Skating Association, 1998

Roy Shipstad

The Skating Scene: Champions & Championships, The Fact Book of Skating
Arthur R. Goodfellow, 1981

Rudy Galindo

Skate Talk: Figure Skating In The Words Of The Stars
Steve Milton, 1998

Icebreaker: The Autobiography Of Rudy Galindo
Rudy Galindo, Eric Marcus, 1997

The Official Book of Figure Skating
U.S. Figure Skating Association, 1998

Culture On Ice: Figure Skating & Cultural Meaning
Ellyn Kestnbaum, 2003

Rupert Whitehead

Unstoppable Energy, Unshakable Faith: An Autobiography
Rupert Whitehead, 2000

Ryan Bradley

Figure Skating Today: The Next Wave of Stars
Steve Milton, Gérard Châtaigneau, 2007

Sally-Anne Stapleford

Skate Talk: Figure Skating In The Words Of The Stars
Steve Milton, 1998

Sandra Bezic

The Passion To Skate: An Intimate View Of Figure Skating
Sandra Bezic, 1996, though it looks at skating as a whole, this book has autobiographical elements

Taking The Ice: Success Stories from the World of Canadian Figure Skating
PJ Kwong, 2010

Sarah Abitbol and Stéphane Bernadis

Un Si Long Silence
Sarah Abitbol, Emmanuelle Anizon, 2020, French language book

Rêve de glace : Drames, passions et secrets du patinage artistique
Sarah Abitbol, Stéphane Bernadis, 2002, French language book

Ice Stars: A Celebration of the Artistry, Beauty and

Grace of the Ice-Skating World
Kevin Bursey, 1999

Sarah Hughes

Figure Skating Champions
Steve Milton, 2002, children's/young adult book

Sudden Champion: The Sarah Hughes Story
Richard Krawiec, 2002, children's/young adult book

Going For The Gold: Sarah Hughes, America's Sweetheart
R.S. Ashby, 2002, children's/young adult book

Sarah Hughes: Skating To The Stars
Alina Sivorinovsky, 2001

Sarah Kawahara

Talking Figure Skating: Behind The Scenes in the World's Most Glamourous Sport
Beverley Smith, 1997

Sarah Meier

Figure Skating Today: The Next Wave of Stars
Steve Milton, Gérard Châtaigneau, 2007

Sasha Cohen

Figure Skating Champions

Steve Milton, Gérard Châtaigneau, 2002, children's/young adult book

Fire On Ice: Autobiography Of A Champion Figure Skater
Sasha Cohen, Amanda Maciel, 2005

Sports Heroes and Legends: Sasha Cohen
Anne E. Hill, 2007, children's/young adult book

Scott Davis

Ice Skating: From Axels to Zambonis
Dan Gutman, 1995, children's/young adult book

Super Skaters: World Figure Skating Stars
Steve Milton, 1994, children's/young adult book

Scott Gregory

Champion Mindset: Refusing To Give Up Your Dreams
Scott Gregory, Candy Abbott, 2020, self-help book with autobiographical elements

Scott Hamilton

Ice Skating: From Axels to Zambonis
Dan Gutman, 1995, children's/young adult book

Ice Cream: Thirty of the Most Interesting Skaters in History
Toller Cranston, Martha Lowder Kimball, 2002

Figure Skating's Greatest Stars
Steve Milton, 2009

Scott Hamilton, Skating For Gold: A Behind The Scenes Look At The Life And Competitive Times Of America's Favorite Figure Skater: An Unauthorized Biography
Michael Steere, 1985

Scott Hamilton
Kristine Brennan, 1999, children's/young adult book

Landing It: My Life On And Off The Ice
Scott Hamilton, Lorenzo Benet, 1999

Scott Hamilton: Fireworks On Ice
Linda Shaughnessy, 1997, children's/young adult book

Finish First: Winning Changes Everything
Scott Hamilton, 2018

Scott Hamilton: Star Figure Skater
Barry Wilner, 1999, children's/young adult book

Ice Stars: A Celebration of the Artistry, Beauty and Grace of the Ice-Skating World
Kevin Bursey, 1999

The Great Eight: How To Be Happy (Even When You Have Every Reason To Be Miserable)
Scott Hamilton, Ken Baker, 2008

The Official Book of Figure Skating
U.S. Figure Skating Association, 1998

Sergei Chetverukhin

Talking Figure Skating: Behind The Scenes in the World's Most Glamourous Sport
Beverley Smith, 1997

Shae-Lynn Bourne and Victor Kraatz

Figure Skating: A Celebration
Beverley Smith, 1994

Figure Skating's Greatest Stars
Steve Milton, 2009

Super Skaters: World Figure Skating Stars
Steve Milton, 1994, children's/young adult book

Skate Talk: Figure Skating In The Words Of The Stars
Steve Milton, 1998

Figure Skating Champions
Steve Milton, Gérard Châtaigneau, 2002, children's/young adult book

Ice Stars: A Celebration of the Artistry, Beauty and Grace of the Ice-Skating World
Kevin Bursey, 1999

Taking The Ice: Success Stories from the World of

Canadian Figure Skating
PJ Kwong, 2010

Sheldon Galbraith

Figure Skating: A Celebration
Beverley Smith, 1994

Minto: Skating Through Time, History of the Minto Skating Club 1904-2004
Janet B. Uren, 2004

Taking The Ice: Success Stories from the World of Canadian Figure Skating
PJ Kwong, 2010

Shizuka Arakawa

15歳の寺子屋 乗り越える力
Shizuka Arakawa, 2011, Japanese language book

フィギュアスケートを100倍楽しく見る方法
Shizuka Arakawa, 2009, Japanese language book

上村愛子物語・荒川静香物語・本橋麻里物語—Legend of the athlete
Shueisha, 2007, Japanese language book

金メダルへの道
Japan Broadcasting Publishing Association, 2006, Japanese language book

氷上のアーティストたち: 日本フィギュアスケートトリノを目指す銀盤の選手たち
Junko Yaginuma, 2005, Japanese language book

Tira mi su 〜だから私はがんばれる！
Kadokawa Shoten, 2006, Japanese language book

Shoma Uno

宇野昌磨 ニューヒーロー 銀メダルへの軌跡
Kodansha, 2018, Japanese language photo book

Sissy Schwarz and Kurt Oppelt

Traumfabrik auf dem Eis: Von der Wiener Eisrevue zu Holiday on Ice
Bernhard Hachleitner, Isabella Lechner, 2014, German language book

Sjoukje Dijkstra

Figure Skating's Greatest Stars
Steve Milton, 2009

Op de schaats
H.J. Looman, 1961, Dutch language book

Triumph auf dem Eis
Heinz Maegerlein, 1964, German language book

Sonia Bianchetti Garbato

Cracked Ice: Figure Skating's Inner World
Sonia Bianchetti Garbato, 2004

Sonja Henie

Henie i Hollywood
Mona Pedersen, 2002, Norwegian language book

Ice Skating: From Axels to Zambonis
Dan Gutman, 1995, children's/young adult book

Figure Skating: A Celebration
Beverley Smith, 1994

Ice Cream: Thirty of the Most Interesting Skaters in History
Toller Cranston, Martha Lowder Kimball, 2002

Figure Skating's Greatest Stars
Steve Milton, 2009

Talking Figure Skating: Behind The Scenes in the World's Most Glamourous Sport
Beverley Smith, 1997

Store fredelige slag
Finn Amundsen, 1941, Norwegian language book

Figure Skating to Fancy Skating: Memoirs of the Life of Sonja Henie
Michael Kirby, 2000

Sonja Henie: Queen Of Ice, Queen of Shadows (later released as Sonja Henie: An Unsuspected Life)
Raymond Strait, Leif Henie, 1990

Wings On My Feet
Sonja Henie, 1940

Ice Stars: A Celebration of the Artistry, Beauty and Grace of the Ice-Skating World
Kevin Bursey, 1999

The Official Book of Figure Skating
U.S. Figure Skating Association, 1998

Earl's Court
Claude Langdon, 1953

Die Eisparade: Meisterinnen auf Schlittschuhen, wie sie sind und wie sie wurden, Kampf um den Weltmeisterthron
Hans Saalbach, 1938, German language book

Ice Skating
T.D. Richardson, 1956

Ice-Skating: A History
Nigel Brown, 1959

Reader's Guide To Figure Skating's Hall of Fame
Benjamin T. Wright, Gregory Smith, U.S. Figure Skating Association, 1978

Skaters' Cavalcade: Fifty Years of Skating
A.C.A. Wade, 1939

The Skating Scene: Champions & Championships, The Fact Book of Skating
Arthur R. Goodfellow, 1981

The Ice Skating Book
Robert Sheffield, Richard Woodward, 1980

Les Riches Heures du Patinage
Jean-Christophe Berlot, 2002, French language book

Whatever Became Of?
Richard Lamparski, 1967

Som i en drøm: Sonja Henies liv
Alf G. Andersen, 1985, Norwegian language book

Hennes form: Sonja Henie 1912-1969
Gunhild Varvin, Henie Onstad Kunstsenter, 2021, Norwegian language book

Sonja Henie
Reidar Børjeson, Henie Onstad Kunstsenter, 1990, Norwegian language book

Sophie Moniotte and Pascal Lavanchy

Les patins de la colère
Sophie Moniotte, Anne Carrière, 1999, French language book

Stanislav Zhuk

Talking Figure Skating: Behind The Scenes in the World's Most Glamourous Sport
Beverley Smith, 1997

…и серебряный иней…
Stanislav Zhuk, 1971, Russian language book

Stéphane Lambiel

Figure Skating Today: The Next Wave of Stars
Steve Milton, Gérard Châtaigneau, 2007

Stéphane Lambiel

Stéphane Lambiel - Le petit prince devenu roi
Félix Clément, Jacques Wullschleger, 2005

Stephanie Westerfeld

Indelible Tracings: The Story of the 1961 U.S. World Figure Skating Team
Patricia Shelley Bushman, 2010

Indelible Images: An Illustrated History Of The 1961 U.S. World Figure Skating Team
Patricia Shelley Bushman, 2011

Frozen in Time: The Enduring Legacy of the 1961 U.S. Figure Skating Team

Nikki Nichols, 2008

Stephen Carriere

Figure Skating Today: The Next Wave of Stars
Steve Milton, Gérard Châtaigneau, 2007

Steven Cousins

Skate Talk: Figure Skating In The Words Of The Stars
Steve Milton, 1998

Steven Cousins

Ice Stars: A Celebration of the Artistry, Beauty and Grace of the Ice-Skating World
Kevin Bursey, 1999

Surya Bonaly

Figure Skating: A Celebration
Beverley Smith, 1994

Talking Figure Skating: Behind The Scenes in the World's Most Glamourous Sport
Beverley Smith, 1997

Super Skaters: World Figure Skating Stars
Steve Milton, 1994, children's/young adult book

Fearless Heart: An Illustrated Biography of Surya Bonaly

Frank Murphy, Surya Bonaly, 2022, children's/young adult book

Surya Bonaly: L'enfant du soleil
Isabelle Rivière, Surya Bonaly. 1995, French language book

Ice Stars: A Celebration of the Artistry, Beauty and Grace of the Ice-Skating World
Kevin Bursey, 1999

Les Riches Heures du Patinage
Jean-Christophe Berlot, 2002, French language book

Susan Humphreys

Talking Figure Skating: Behind The Scenes in the World's Most Glamourous Sport
Beverley Smith, 1997

Skate Talk: Figure Skating In The Words Of The Stars
Steve Milton, 1998

Susanna Rahkamo and Petri Kokko

Susanna ja Petri - Unelmista totta
Sussanna Rahkamo, Petri Kokko, Anu Puromies, 1995, Finnish language book

Suzanne Morrow and Wally Distelmeyer

Figure Skating: A Celebration

Beverley Smith, 1994

Talking Figure Skating: Behind The Scenes in the World's Most Glamourous Sport
Beverley Smith, 1997

T.D. Richardson

Reader's Guide To Figure Skating's Hall of Fame
Benjamin T. Wright, Gregory Smith, U.S. Figure Skating Association, 1978

Our Skating Heritage
Dennis L. Bird, 1979

Tai Babilonia and Randy Gardner

Still Skating Forward: Amazing People Celebrating Life and Skating
Joanne Vossallo Jamrosz, 2012

Playing It Straight : Personal Conversations on Recovery, Transformation and Success
David Dodd, 1992, book on recovery that profiles Tai Babilonia

Ballet on Ice: The Story of Tai Babilonia and Randy Gardner
Elizabeth Wheeler, 1981

Forever Two As One
Tai Babilonia, Randy Gardner, Martha Lowder Kimball,

2002

The Official Book of Figure Skating
U.S. Figure Skating Association, 1998

Takahiko Kozuka

フィギュアスケート 氷の上で感じた世界
Takahiko Kozuka, 2019, Japanese language book

ステップ バイ ステップ
Takahiko Kozuka, Bungei Shunju, 2012, Japanese language book

Takahiko
Hidemi Ogata, 2011, Japanese language photo book

Takeshi Honda

氷上のアーティストたち: 日本フィギュアスケートトリノを目指す銀盤の選手たち
Junko Yaginuma, 2005, Japanese language book

Ice Stars: A Celebration of the Artistry, Beauty and Grace of the Ice-Skating World
Kevin Bursey, 1999

Tamara Moskvina and Igor Moskvin

Слезы на льду
Elena Vaitsekhovskaya, 2007, Russian language book

Москвины. Лед для двоих
Elena Vaitsekhovskaya, 2011, Russian language book

Tanith Belbin and Benjamin Agosto

Figure Skating Today: The Next Wave of Stars
Steve Milton, Gérard Châtaigneau, 2007

Tanja Szewczenko

Durch die Hölle zum Glück
Tanja Szewczenko, 2022, health related German language book that contains autobiographical elements

Ice Stars: A Celebration of the Artistry, Beauty and Grace of the Ice-Skating World
Kevin Bursey, 1999

Tara Lipinski

Stories Of Triumph: Women Who Win In Sport and Life
Christine Lessa, 1998

Talking Figure Skating: Behind The Scenes in the World's Most Glamourous Sport
Beverley Smith, 1997

Skate Talk: Figure Skating In The Words Of The Stars
Steve Milton, 1998

Tara And Michelle: The Road To Gold

Wendy Daly, 1997, children's/young adult book

Tara Lipinski: Queen Of The Ice
Bill Gutman, 1999, children's/young adult book

On The Ice With... Tara Lipinski
Matt Christopher, 1999, children's/young adult book

Tara Lipinski, Superstar Ice Skater
Stasia Ward Kehoe, 2001, children's/young adult book

Tara Lipinski: Olympic Champion
Cynthia Benjamin, 2002, children's/young adult book

Tara Lipinski
Terri Dougherty, 1999, children's/young adult book

Tara Lipinski
Jill Wheeler, 1998, children's/young adult book

Tara Lipinski
Richard Rambeck, 1999, children's/young adult book

Tara Lipinski (Champion Sport Biographies)
Annis Karpenko, 1999, children's/young adult book

Skating For The Gold: Michelle Kwan & Tara Lipinski
Chip Lovitt, 1997, children's/young adult book

Tara Lipinski: Star Figure Skater
Barry Wilner, 2001, children's/young adult book

Triumph On Ice: An Autobiography
Tara Lipinski, Emily Costello, 1997, children's/young adult book

Totally Tara: An Olympic Journey
Tara Lipinski, Mark Zeigler, 1998, children's/young adult book

Ice Stars: A Celebration of the Artistry, Beauty and Grace of the Ice-Skating World
Kevin Bursey, 1999

The Official Book of Figure Skating
U.S. Figure Skating Association, 1998

Tatiana Malinina

Ice Stars: A Celebration of the Artistry, Beauty and Grace of the Ice-Skating World
Kevin Bursey, 1999

Tatiana Navka and Roman Kostomarov

Слезы на льду
Elena Vaitsekhovskaya, 2007, Russian language book

Фигурное катание. Только звезды
Elena Vaitsekhovskaya, Alexander Wilf, 2008, Russian language book

Tatiana Tarasova

Четыре времени года
Tatiana Tarasova, 1985, Russian language book

Слезы на льду
Elena Vaitsekhovskaya, 2007, Russian language book

Красавица и чудовище
Tatiana Tarasova, 2008, Russian language book

Tatiana Totmianina and Maxim Marinin

Две стороны одной медали
Tatiana Totmianina, Maxim Marinin, 2018, Russian language book

Tatiana Volosozhar and Maxim Trankov

Татьяна Волосожар и Максим Траньков. Две стороны одной медали
Tatiana Volosozhar, Maxim Trankov, 2018, Russian language book

Tatsuki Machida

そこに音楽がある限り──フィギュアスケーター・町田樹の軌跡
Tatsuki Machida, Shinshokan, 2019, Japanese language book

アイスモデリスト
Junko Yaginuma, 2012, Japanese language book

Tenley Albright

Ice Skating: From Axels to Zambonis
Dan Gutman, 1995, children's/young adult book

Figure Skating's Greatest Stars
Steve Milton, 2009

The Official Book of Figure Skating
U.S. Figure Skating Association, 1998

The Skating Scene: Champions & Championships, The Fact Book of Skating
Arthur R. Goodfellow, 1981

Tessa Virtue and Scott Moir

Figure Skating Today: The Next Wave of Stars
Steve Milton, Gérard Châtaigneau, 2007

Tessa And Scott: Our Journey From Childhood Dream To Olympic Gold
Tessa Virtue, Scott Moir, Steve Milton, 2010

Taking The Ice: Success Stories from the World of Canadian Figure Skating
PJ Kwong, 2010

Theresa Weld Blanchard and Nathaniel Niles

The First Twenty-Five Years of the United States Figure Skating Association 1921-1946
U.S. Figure Skating Association, 1946

The Skating Scene: Champions & Championships, The Fact Book of Skating
Arthur R. Goodfellow, 1981

Reader's Guide To Figure Skating's Hall of Fame
Benjamin T. Wright, Gregory Smith, U.S. Figure Skating Association, 1978

Tiffany Chin

Tiffany Chin: A Dream On Ice
Ray Buck, 1986, children's/young adult book

Tiffany Scott and Philip Dulebohn

Skating With The World
Joanne Vassallo Jamrosz, 2014

Timothy Goebel

Figure Skating Champions
Steve Milton, Gérard Châtaigneau, 2002, children's/young adult book

Ice Stars: A Celebration of the Artistry, Beauty and Grace of the Ice-Skating World
Kevin Bursey, 1999

Todd Eldredge

Talking Figure Skating: Behind The Scenes in the

World's Most Glamourous Sport
Beverley Smith, 1997

Skate Talk: Figure Skating In The Words Of The Stars
Steve Milton, 1998

Figure Skating Champions
Steve Milton, Gérard Châtaigneau, 2002,
children's/young adult book

Gold! The Todd Eldredge Story
Alicia Styles, 2000

Ice Stars: A Celebration of the Artistry, Beauty and
Grace of the Ice-Skating World
Kevin Bursey, 1999

The Official Book of Figure Skating
U.S. Figure Skating Association, 1998

Toller Cranston

Figure Skating: A Celebration
Beverley Smith, 1994

Figure Skating's Greatest Stars
Steve Milton, 2009

The Golden Age of Canadian Figure Skating
David Young, 1984

Skate Talk: Figure Skating In The Words Of The Stars

Steve Milton, 1998

Remembering Toller Cranston: Memoir Of A Friendship Between Two Artists
Andrew Osta, 2017

Ice Cream: Thirty Of The Most Interesting Skaters In History
Toller Cranston, Martha Lowder Kimball, 2002, while mostly about other skaters, does include anecdotes about Toller

When Hell Freezes Over: Should I Bring My Skates?
Toller Cranston, Martha Lowder Kimball, 2000

Zero Tollerance: An Intimate Memoir By The Man Who Revolutionized Figure Skating
Toller Cranston, Martha Lowder Kimball, 1997

Toller
Elva Oglanby, 1976

The Official Book of Figure Skating
U.S. Figure Skating Association, 1998

Taking The Ice: Success Stories from the World of Canadian Figure Skating
PJ Kwong, 2010

Toller: Ice
Robert Hughes, Hughes Brittle Printing, 2019, lined notebook with quotes

Toller: Beginnings
Robert Hughes, Hughes Brittle Printing, 2019, lined notebook with quotes

Tomáš Verner

Figure Skating Today: The Next Wave of Stars
Steve Milton, Gérard Châtaigneau, 2007

Tonia Kwiatkowski

Skate Talk: Figure Skating In The Words Of The Stars
Steve Milton, 1998

Tonya Harding

Figure Skating: A Celebration
Beverley Smith, 1994

Ice Cream: Thirty of the Most Interesting Skaters in History
Toller Cranston, Martha Lowder Kimball, 2002

Thin Ice: The Complete, Uncensored Story of Tonya Harding
Nellie Coffey, Joseph Layden, Frank Coffey, 1994

Women on Ice: Feminist Responses to the Tonya Harding/Nancy Kerrigan Spectacle
Cynthia Baughman, 1995

The Tonya Tapes: The Tonya Harding Story In Her Own Voice
Tonya Harding, Lynda Prouse, 2008, second edition released in 2017

Fire On Ice: The Exclusive Inside Story Of Tonya Harding
Abby Haight, J.E. Vader, 1994

Les Riches Heures du Patinage
Jean-Christophe Berlot, 2002, French language book

Toshikazu Kagiyama

氷鬼—片山敏一先生古稀記念
Ice Rainbow Club Secretariat, 1983, Japanese language book

Tracy Wilson and Rob McCall

Skate: 100 Years Of Figure Skating
Steve Milton, Barbara McCutcheon, 1996

The Top 15: Nova Scotia's Greatest Athletes
Nova Scotia Sport Hall of Fame, 2018

Taking The Ice: Success Stories from the World of Canadian Figure Skating
PJ Kwong, 2010

Skate Talk: Figure Skating In The Words Of The Stars
Steve Milton, 1998

Trixi Schuba

Ice Cream: Thirty of the Most Interesting Skaters in History
Toller Cranston, Martha Lowder Kimball, 2002

Trixi Schuba: Die Kür meines Lebens
Trixi Schuba, 2016, German language book

Trixie the Skating Juggler

Trixie: Child Prodigy, Skating Star and Juggling Icon
David Cain, 2017

Ulrich Salchow

Ice Stars: A Celebration of the Artistry, Beauty and Grace of the Ice-Skating World
Kevin Bursey, 1999

Ice Skating
T.D. Richardson, 1956

Reader's Guide To Figure Skating's Hall of Fame
Benjamin T. Wright, Gregory Smith, U.S. Figure Skating Association, 1978

The Skating Scene: Champions & Championships, The Fact Book of Skating
Arthur R. Goodfellow, 1981

Uschi Keszler

Skate Talk: Figure Skating In The Words Of The Stars
Steve Milton, 1998

Vern Lundquist

Skate Talk: Figure Skating In The Words Of The Stars
Steve Milton, 1998

Viktor Petrenko

Ice Skating: From Axels to Zambonis
Dan Gutman, 1995, children's/young adult book

Vivi-Anne Hultén

Die Eisparade: Meisterinnen auf Schlittschuhen, wie sie sind und wie sie wurden, Kampf um den Weltmeisterthron
Hans Saalbach, 1938, German language book

Walter S. Powell

Indelible Tracings: The Story of the 1961 U.S. World Figure Skating Team
Patricia Shelley Bushman, 2010

Indelible Images: An Illustrated History Of The 1961 U.S. World Figure Skating Team
Patricia Shelley Bushman, 2011

Frozen in Time: The Enduring Legacy of the 1961 U.S. Figure Skating Team
Nikki Nichols, 2008

The First Twenty-Five Years of the United States Figure Skating Association 1921-1946
U.S. Figure Skating Association, 1946

Werner Groebli and Hansruedi Mauch (Frick and Frack)

Swiss Movements: An American Dream, The autobiography of Mr. Frick
Werner Groebli, Thomas Foeldi, 2016

Figure Skating's Greatest Stars
Steve Milton, 2009

Wilhelm Henie

Lille Sonjas store pappa
Tor Bomann-Larsen, 1993, Norwegian language children's/young adult book

Willy Böckl

Reader's Guide To Figure Skating's Hall of Fame
Benjamin T. Wright, Gregory Smith, U.S. Figure Skating Association, 1978

150 Jahre Eiszeit: Die Grosse Geschichte des Wiener Eislauf-Vereines
Agnes Meisinger, 2017, German language book

Xue Shen and Hongbo Zhao

Figure Skating's Greatest Stars
Steve Milton, 2009

Figure Skating Today: The Next Wave of Stars
Steve Milton, Gérard Châtaigneau, 2007

Ice Stars: A Celebration of the Artistry, Beauty and Grace of the Ice-Skating World
Kevin Bursey, 1999

Yukari Nakano

Figure Skating Today: The Next Wave of Stars
Steve Milton, Gérard Châtaigneau, 2007

Figure Skating Today: The Next Wave of Stars
Steve Milton, Gérard Châtaigneau, 2007

Yuna Kim: Ice Queen
Christine Dzidrums, Leah Rendon, 2011, children's/young adult book

한 번의 비상을 위한 천 번의 점프
Brian Orser, translated and published by Woongjin Jisik House, 2009, Korean language book

도전! 슈퍼코리언 김연아
Junior JoongAng Books, Korean language children's/young adult book

신동들의 비밀 수첩 : 피겨 신동 김연아에서 수영 신동 박태환까지
Lee Na-young and Lee Jeong-eun, 2007, Korean language children's/young adult book

아이의 재능에 꿈의 날개를 달아라
Park Mi-hee, 2008, Korean language book

체육인 27인의 감동 수기 : 그대들이 있어 대한민국은 행복합니다
Korea Sports Promotion Agency, 2008, Korean language book

김연아처럼
Yuna Kim, Korean language children's/young adult book

김연아의 7분 드라마
Yuna Kim, 2010, Korean language book

Yuzuru Hanyu

「YUZURU Ⅲ 羽生結弦写真集」
Nao Noto, Shueisha, 2022, Japanese language photo book

「羽生結弦 SEASON PHOTOBOOK 2021-2022」
Nobuaki Tanaka, Rudder, 2022, Japanese language photo book

「羽生結弦　2021-2022」
Toru Yaguchi, Sports Report, 2022, Japanese language

photo book

「羽生結弦写真集　ENDLESS DREAM －果てなき夢－ 2021-2022シーズン最新フォト満載！」
Jin Mochizuki, Afro Koichi Nakamura, 2022, Japanese language photo book

「YUZU'LL BE BACK IV 羽生結弦写真集2021〜2022」
Toyoshiki Koumi, Yutaka Nagakubo, Toshiyuki Kojima, Sports Nippon Shimbun, 2022, Japanese language photo book

「羽生結弦 北京オリンピック2022 フォトブック」
Nobuaki Tanaka, Rudder, 2022, Japanese language photo book

「羽生結弦POSTCARD BOOK "Hearts"」
Tokyo News Service, 2022, Japanese language photo book

「羽生結弦 SEASON PHOTOBOOK 2020-2021」
Nobuaki Tanaka, Rudder, 2021, Japanese language photo book

「羽生結弦写真集REGROWTH リグロウス－再生－」
Afro Koichi Nakamura, Kosaido Publishing, 2021, Japanese language photo book

「YUZU'LL BE BACK III 羽生結弦写真集2020〜2021」
Toramoto Koumi, Yutaka Nagakubo, Sports Nippon Shimbun, 2021, Japanese language photo book

「羽生結弦写真集 The Real 美しき練習着の勇姿」
Nao Noto, Yuji Taguchi, Kobashi Castle, Mountains and Valleys, 2021, Japanese language photo book

「羽生結弦大型写真集 光 −Be the Light−
Nao Noto, Shueisha, 2021, Japanese language photo book

YUZU'LL BE BACK〜Dancin' on The Edge 3
Toramoto Koumi, Yutaka Nagakubo, Sports Nippon Shimbun, 2020, Japanese language photo book

「羽生結弦　2019-2020」
Toru Yaguchi, Sports Report, 2020, Japanese language photo book

「羽生結弦 SEASON PHOTOBOOK 2019-2020」
Nobuaki Tanaka, Rudder, 2020, Japanese language photo book

「羽生結弦 SEASON PHOTOBOOK 2018-2019」
Nobuaki Tanaka, Kadashisha, 2019, Japanese language photo book

YUZU'LL BE BACK〜Dancin' on The Edge 2
Toramoto Koumi, Yutaka Nagakubo, Sports Nippon Shimbun, 2018, Japanese language photo book

「YUZURU II 羽生結弦写真集」
Nao Noto, Shueisha, 2018, Japanese language photo book

「羽生結弦 平昌オリンピック2018 フォトブック」
Shinshokan, 2018, Japanese language photo book

「羽生結弦 平昌オリンピック2018 フォトブック」
Nobuaki Tanaka, Rudder, 2018, Japanese language photo book

「羽生結弦 SEASON PHOTOBOOK 2017-2018」
Nobuaki Tanaka, Rudder, 2018, Japanese language photo book

「羽生結弦 SEASON PHOTOBOOK 2016-2017」
Nobuaki Tanaka, Rudder, 2017, Japanese language photo book

「羽生結弦 SEASON PHOTOBOOK 2015-2016」
Nobuaki Tanaka, Rudder, 2016, Japanese language photo book

「YUZURU 羽生結弦写真集」
Nao Noto, Shueisha, 2014, Japanese language photo book

羽生結弦　アマチュア時代　全記録
CCC Media House, 2022, Japanese language book

『羽生結弦　飛躍の原動力』プレミアム保存版
AERA Editorial Department, 2022, Japanese language book

共に、前へ 羽生結弦 東日本大震災10年の記憶
Shodensha, 2021, Japanese language book

羽生結弦ダイアリー 〜ALWAYS WITH YUZU〜
Nobuaki Tanaka, Rudder, 2021, Japanese language book

羽生結弦 王者のメソッド 2008-2016
Mie Noguchi, 2016, Japanese language book

羽生結弦 未来をつくる
Yuzuru Hanyu, Shueisha, 2021, Japanese language book

夢を生きる
Yuzuru Hanyu, Takarajimasha, 2020, Japanese language book

夢を生きる
Yuzuru Hanyu, Chuokoron Shinsha, 2018, Japanese language book

羽生結弦語録
Yuzuru Hanyu, Pia, 2015, Japanese language book

蒼い炎II－飛翔編
Yuzuru Hanyu, Fusosha, 2016, Japanese language book

蒼い炎
Yuzuru Hanyu, Fusosha, 2012, Japanese language book

アイスモデリスト
Junko Yaginuma, 2012, Japanese language book

NEWSPAPERS

The fact is, the mainstream media has done a remarkable job at covering figure skating over the years. Where would we be without Beverley Smith's wonderful articles for "The Globe and Mail" or the extensive coverage of the sport's early history in Europe in publications like the "Wiener Sportagblatt"? Mainstream newspapers, lifestyle and sporting magazines and journals are all rich sources of information worth exploring and the great news is that you find archives of many of them online – some free, some not.

Start by reaching out to your local library to see if they have a subscription to ProQuest. In terms of free resources, it's one of the best out there. After you've given ProQuest a go, start your trip around the world by exploring some of these extensive newspaper databases.

ANNO
Austria
Free

BANQ
Canada
Free

British Newspaper Archive
United Kingdom
Pay

CDNC
United States
Free

Europeana
Germany, Netherlands, Austria, Latvia, Estonia, Finland, Serbia, Poland
Free

Fulton History
United States
Free

Gallica
France
Free

Kansalliskirjasto
Finland
Free

Nasjonalbiblioteket
Norway
Free*

National Diet Library
Japan
Free*

NewspaperArchive.com
Canada, United States, United Kingdom, South Africa, France, Germany

Pay

Newspapers.com
Canada, United States, United Kingdom
Pay
Papers Past
New Zealand
Free

Svenska Dagbladet
Sweden
Pay

TimesMachine
United States
Pay

Trove
Australia
Free

*international access limited

PERIODICALS

I consulted a wide range of sources when compiling this alphabetical directory of skating periodicals, but I want to specifically acknowledge a few significant sources of information:

- *Lists of skating periodicals compiled by German skating historian Dr. Matthias Hampe and photographer J. Barry Mittan*

- *Lennart Månsson, who shared her extensive knowledge of Swedish skating periodicals*

- *"Our Skating Heritage", Dennis L. Bird (1979)*

- *"The Skater's Edge Sourcebook", Alice Berman (1994)*

In addition to this extensive listing, I also want to point out the fact that many skating clubs, sections and regions around the world have produced their own newsletters over the years. If you're looking for information on a particular skater, I would first determine which club they skated out of and if it still exists, reach out to them to see if they have kept issues of any club newsletters from the time period they competed.

In the 1980's and early 1990's, the majority of the world's top figure skaters also had fan clubs that posted newsletters to members. Brian Boitano fans could sign up to receive a copy of "Outside Edges"; Kurt

Browning lovers got their fix with the "What A Wonderful World". At one point, there were two different Brian Orser newsletters - "Orser's Endorsers" and Trudi A. Marrapodi's "The Lion Sleeps", which operated for eight years. When the internet became increasingly popular in the mid-to-late nineties, the majority of these print newsletters transitioned to web pages or went defunct.

6.0 Figure Skating Magazine
Ukraine
Circa 1996-1997, stopped publication by 2002

A jég
Hungary
1920's
Budapesti Korcsolyázó Egylet

American Skating World
United States
April 1981-June 2000
Business Communications Inc. (Michael E. Romanus Jr., editor H. Kermit Jackson)

Annual USFSA Yearbook: The Standard Reference Book of American Figure Skating
United States
1940-1943 (3 issues)
U.S. Figure Skating Association

Aussie Skates

Australia
E-zine from 2005 to present
Nick Pilgrim

Blade Runners
United States
First issue in 2000
Mary Sinker

Blades on Ice
United States
1990-Spring 2011 (moved to online only and went defunct soon after)
Gerri Walbert

Bulletin du Club des Patineurs
France
1908 (3 issues)
Club des Patineurs de Paris

C.O.S.S.I.P. (later Celebrating Our Section)
Canada
First issue in early 1960's. First issue of pared-down Celebrating Our Section newsletter published in 1994.
Central Ontario Section, CFSA/Skate Canada

Canadian Blades
Canada
Circa 1996-2002

Canadian Figure Skating
Canada

1986
Canadian Figure Skating Association

Canadian Skate newletter
United States
First issue circa 1996-1997. Stopped publication by 2002.
Carol Gilbert

Der Eiskunstlauf
Germany

Deutschen Eislauf-Union
Der Eissport
Germany
First issue in 1920's, after 45 issues renamed in 1933 to "Der weiße Sport" ("The white sport") during The Third Reich. Based in Berlin.

Deutscher Eislaufverband
Der Eissport
Germany
First issue in 1953. Based in Düsseldorf.

Fachorgan des Deutschen Eissportes
Der Eissport
Germany
First issue in 1957. Based in München.

Deutschen Eissportverbandes
Der Schweizer Eislauf
Switzerland
First issue in 1978. Based in Wintherhur

Schwager Der Schweizer Eissport
Switzerland
First issue in 1933
Schweizer Eislauf-Verbandes

Der Winter
Germany
Published in Munich, circa 1914

DEU-Informationen (later DEU-Press)
Germany
First issue 1989
Deutschen Eislauf-Union

Deutscher Eis-Sport
Germany
First issue 1901, 11 issues total. Based in München.
Deutsch-Österreichischen Eislaufverbandes

Deutscher Eissport
Germany
First issue 1966, 9 issues in total. Based in Berlin.
Deutschen Eissportverbandes

Deutscher Wintersport
Germany
Published in Berlin, first issue circa 1914, 32 issues total, renamed in 1922
Deutschen Eislaufverbandes

Doppio Axel

Italy
First issue 2006
Simone Ramella, Chiara Canensi

Eislaufinformationen
Switzerland
Schweizer Eislauf-Verbandes

Eissport-Magazin
Germany
January 1993-October 2009. Based in Cologne.
Dr. Sepp Schönmetzler

Eis-und-Rollsport
Germany
Last issue 1941-1942, 52 issues total
Limpert, DrfL (specialist office for ice and roller sports, Deutschen Eislaufverband during The Third Reich)

Eis-und-Rollsport
Germany
First issue in 1950. Based in Hamburg. Trade journal for figure skating, ice dance, hockey and speed skating.

ESPA-News
Germany
First issue in 1993
European Professional Skating Coaches Association

Figure Skater Fitness
Canada
October 2015-present

Flexafit (Signe Ronka)

Finsk Idrottsblad (later Idrottsbladet)
Finland
1904-1947. Merged with Svenska Finlands Idrottsförbundin's "Idrott magazine" in 1937. Though a multi-sport magazine, was the official publication of the Suomen Luistinliitto
Helsingfors gymnastikklubb

Freestyle
United States
Circa 1995-1996
Emma Abraham

Ghiacciosport
Italy
1995-1996

Glaciettes
Australia
1936-1939
Melbourne Glaciarium

Glint zine
Canada
1997-1998
Yasmin Siddiqui, Jenny Tong

Go Figure!
United States
June 1999-April 2002

Castine Communications (Julie Nikolovski)

Gotta Skate
United States
Circa 1995. Stopped publication by 2002.

ICE
Russia
Circa 2010-2011

Ice Age
United Kingdom
1994-1996
Denbigh Publications

Ice and Blade
Canada

Ice Castle News
United States
First issue in 1990
Ice Castle (Lake Arrowhead, CA)

Ice Chips
Canada
Circa early 1960's
Prairie and Saskatchewan Sections, CFSA/Skate Canada

Ice Chronicles
United States
1996-1997

Ice Cycles
United States
1987-1990
Ice Cycles Inc. (Tampa, FL)

Ice Link
United Kingdom
Circa 1996-1997
National Ice Skating Association

Ice Prints
United States
1989-1991
New York Regional Council of Figure Skating Clubs (NYRCFSC)

Ice Skating
United Kingdom
1946-1947, allied with Skating World
Cyril Beastall

Ice Skating Magazine (later 6.0 Skate Magazine)
United States
2002-2004

Ice Skating Down Under
Australia
First published in 1990
National Ice Skating Association of Australia

Ice Skating International Annual
United States

1997-1998 (no longer printing annuals, in continuous operation as an online magazine since 1995)
George S. Rossano

Ice Skating News Graphic
United States
1945-1949
Ice Publications (Lee S. Woodruff)

Ice Tracings
New Zealand
First issue in 1946
New Zealand Ice Skating Association

International Figure Skating
United States
1994-2023
Laurea Media (Susan D. Russell), previously Mavador Media, Paragraph Communications

International Ice Skating Directory
United Kingdom
1951-1952
Phyllis East Publishing Co. Ltd. (Phyllis East)

International Skater
United Kingdom
Diamond Euro Press

ISAI newsletter (later ISI Edge trade journal)
United States
1959-2020

Ice Skating Institute of America

iSKATE
United Kingdom
2006-July 2012
Ice Media Productions (Heath Rhodes)

ISSA Skating News (also Ice Skating in South Africa, S.A. Skating World)
South Africa
September 1991-May 2000 (moved to online only and is still in publication as an e-newsletter)
Irvine Green

ISU World
Switzerland
First issue in 1997
International Skating Union

Keeping In Touch
Canada
Paper issue in February 1997, bifold first issued in early 1990's, later transitioned to online
Canadian Figure Skating Association, Skate Canada

Konståkaren: medlemsblad för svensk konståkning
Sweden
1958-1959
Svenska Konståkningsförbundet

Konståkningsnytt
Sweden

1974-1981
Svenska Konståkningsförbundet

Kunstrijden
Holland

Le Patinage Suisse
Switzerland
Circa 1994
Schweizer Eislauf-Verbandes

Le Patineur: journal illustré spécial
France
October 1894-November 1897
Edmond de Saymar

Les Sports d'hiver
France
1908-1924 (criticized heavily by editors of rival publication for being used as a vehicle for self-promotion)
Louis Magnus

Luistelijia
Finland
Circa 1994

Mitteilungen des Berliner Schlittschuhklubs e.V.
Germany
First issue in 1898

Muse-ings (later Reflections on Ice)

United States
Print newsletters circa 1995, started online newsletter in June 2005
World Figure Skating Museum and Hall of Fame

National Ice News
Australia
First published in 1986
Australian Ice Hockey Federation, Ice Skating Australia

National Ice Skating Guide (later National Ice Skating and Arena Guide, World Ice Skating Guide)
United States
1941-1968
National Sports Publications (Arthur R. Goodfellow, James C. Hendy)

OzSkater
Australia
2003-2018
New South Wales Ice Skating Association

Patinage
France
1986-present
Media Loisirs International

Pattinie e Ghiaccio
Italy
First issue in 1956
Circolo Pattinatori Artistici di Milano

Pirouette
Germany
1968-present
STS Verlag+
Werbung (Petra Wagner, CStefan Schulze)

Piruett
Sweden
1965-1972, 1973-1980 (originally published by Svenska Konståkningsförbundet, then after a conflict published by an independent group with revenue going towards grants for promising Swedish skaters)
Svenska Konståkningsförbundet, later Stiftelsen Piruett

Pirueta
Czech Republic
Český krasobruslařský svaz

Professional Figure Skaters Cooperative newsletter (later The PFSC Post, ProSkaters newsletter)
United States
June 1998-Spring 2011
Professional Figure Skaters Cooperative (Sylvia Froescher, Tamara Sharp)

Puck & Skating
Belgium
Ligue Royale Belge des Sports de Glace

Recreational Ice Skating
United States
Still in publication, first issue was pre-1994

Ice Skating Institute of America

Schaats + Kroniek
Holland
Koninklijke Nederlandsche Schaatsenrijders Bond

Schaatsen: ijzersterk en winterhard magazine voor de schaatsliefhebber
Holland
1997-2001
Telegraaf Tijdschriften Groep

Scottish Skating Update
United Kingdom
Circa 1996-1997
Scottish Ice Skating Association

Skate Six
Canada
1996-1997
Canadian Figure Skating Association

Skaters Edge
United Kingdom
First issue in 1990

Skater's Edge
United States
September-October 1991-Summer 2001
Alice Berman

Skater's Solutions newsletter

United States
Circa 1996-1997

SkateTalk!: The Newsletter by and for Figure Skating Fans
United States
Circa 1995-1997

Skating
United States
December 1923-present
United States Figure Skating Association, U.S. Figure Skating

Skating Monthly's Entertainment Magazine
United States
Circa 1997

Skating News
United Kingdom
Circa 1994

Skating Sketches
United States
September 1995-2000
Kathleen Stafford

Skating World
United Kingdom
1936-1973
Cyril Beastall

Ski & Skate (also Ice & Roller Skate, Skate, Skate Yearbook)
United Kingdom
1970-1986
Joan and Fred Dean

Skøjtesport
Denmark
Circa 1994
Dansk Skøjte Union

Skøytesport
Norway
Circa 1994
Norges Skøyterforbund

Skridsko-Nytt
Sweden
1956-2005, strictly a speed skating magazine with the exception of 1998-1999, when the publication merged with "Svensk Konståkning" briefly, with one half of the magazine devoted to figure skating
Svenska Skridskoförbundet

Slovenian Association of Ice Skating Sports Almanac
Slovenia
Circa 1997-2000
Slovene Skating Union

Spalding's Athletic Library Official Ice Hockey Guide and Winter Sports Almanac
Canada

1921-1924
A.G. Spalding & Bros. of Canada Ltd. (Champlain Provencher)

Sport im Wiener Eislauf-Verein
Austria
First issue in 1927
Wiener Eislauf-Verein

Sports de Neige et Glace (later Sports d'hiver)
France
October 1923-December 1947 (interruption during World War II)
Fédération française des sports d'hiver (A. Maucourt)

Spotlight on Skating
Canada
February 1999-December 2007
G. Lisa Herdman

Suomen Urheilulehti
Finland

Suomen Luistinliitto
Finland

Suomen Tatitoluistelu
Finland
Circa 1994
Suomen Tailotuisteluliitto

Svensk Konståkning

Sweden
1982-1999. 1998-1999 issues were merged with speed skating magazine "Skridsko-Nytt". There was an attempt to make it an online magazine in 1999, but it really just became part of the Svenska Konståkningsförbundet's website.
Svenska Konståkningsförbundet

Synchronized Skating Magazine
United States
Fall 2003-2008

The Canadian Skater
Canada
December 1968-1984
Canadian Figure Skating Association

The Edge newsletter
United States
First issue circa 1996-1997. Stopped publication by 2002.

The Field: The Country Gentleman's Newspaper (later The Field)
United Kingdom
1853-present. Though marketed today as "the best place to read about country and field sports and country life", this publication was endorsed as the official publication of the National Skating Association until the 1930's. T.D. Richardson wrote for them at the time.
Later TI Media (Future plc)

The Figure Skating Journal newsletter

United States
Circa 1996-1997

The Inside Edge
Canada
First issue in 1965
Western Ontario and Niagara Peninsula Section, CFSA

The Journal of the Figure Skating Historical Society
United States
Quarterly from Spring 1994-Winter 1996
Figure Skating Historical Society, Inc. (Jill Eicher)

The Monthly Freeze
United Kingdom
Circa 1927-1930
Miss Ramsden

The Outside Edge
South Africa
Summer 1971-March 1992
South African Ice Skating Association (Irvine Green)

The Professional Skater (PS Magazine)
United States
1969-Present
Professional Skaters Association

The Skater: The Only Journal Devoted Exclusively to Skating
United Kingdom
First issue published in November 1924

The Skater (later The Skater, Skier and Hockey Player, Winter Sports)
United Kingdom
1948-1969
Howard Bass Publications (Howard Bass)

The Skating Review
United Kingdom
Autumn 1935-1937
National Skating Association

The Stage (Ice Supplement)
United Kingdom
1954-1955
The Stage Media Company Ltd.

The Ice Rink and Skating World (later The Skating Times and Winter Sports Illustrated)
United Kingdom
1930-1950 (did not operate during wartime, revived in 1947)
British Continental Press Ltd., The Skating Times Magazine Co. Ltd.

Thin Ice
Canada
First issue in 1963
British Columbia Section, CFSA/Skate Canada

Today's Skating (later Today's Skater)
Canada

1990-1994
Canadian Figure Skating Association

Tracings
United States
1975-2000 (moved to online only and went defunct soon after)
New England Inter-Club Council

White Ice
Australia
Circa 1996-1997 (transitioned to web site in 1998 and went defunct shortly thereafter)

Winter Sports Review (also Winter Sports Annual 1911-12)
United Kingdom
November 1911-1913. Quarterly on skating, curling and skiing published in London.
E.C. Richardson, E. Wroughton

World Figure Skating
Japan
First issue 1999

Yuzuru Hanyu Season Photobook
Japan
2004-present
Nobuaki Tanaka

журнал кI П есть Ноль '6.0'
Russia

First issue in March 1997
Chaikovskaya Skate Ltd. (Elena Chaikovskaya, Alexander Kosterov)

Московский фигурист (Moscow Figure Skater)
Russia
Spring 2006-present
Moscow Figure Skating Federation (Olga Verezemskaya)

Журнал «Ледовое шоу»
Russia
Early 2000's

Фигурное катание
Russia
2001-2008

キス&クライ(Kiss & Cry)
Japan
2013-present
Honto

クワッドアクセル (Quadruple Axel)
Japan
Currently in publication

フィギュアスケートマガジン(Figure Skating Magazine – Trace of Stars)
Japan
Currently in publication

フィギュアスケート人生 (Figure Skating Life)

Japan
Currently in publication
Fusosha (Kaori Okubo)

世界フィギュアスケート (World Figure Skating)
Japan
Currently in publication

氷の宝石 (Ice Jewels)
Japan
Currently in publication

ACKNOWLEDGMENTS

A very special thanks to the following individuals, without whom this book would not have been possible.

Sandra Bezic
Yvonne Butorac
Irvine Green
Dr. Matthias Hampe
Elaine Hooper
Lennart Månsson
Tina Tyan

AUTHOR'S NOTE

Thank you so much for your kind support and interest. I hope that you have found "A Bibliography of Figure Skating" to be a helpful resource!

If so, I would so appreciate it if you took a few moments to write a short honest review on the website of the retailer where you purchased this book.

Reviews make such a huge difference in helping more people discovering books and I do hope you consider taking the time to leave one.

OTHER BOOKS

Jackson Haines: The Skating King

The Almanac of Canadian Figure Skating

Technical Merit: A History of Figure Skating Jumps

www.ingramcontent.com/pod-product-compliance
Lightning Source LLC
LaVergne TN
LVHW051544070426
835507LV00021B/2402